The Mysterious  & Unknown

UFOs

by Gail B. Stewart

ReferencePoint
Press™

San Diego, CA

For more information, contact
ReferencePoint Press, Inc.
PO Box 27779
San Diego, CA 92198
www.ReferencePointPress.com

Picture credits:

Maury Aaseng, 16, 34, 47
AP/Wide World Photos, 27, 40, 80
Dreamstime, 6, 9, 12, 20, 25, 49, 58, 64
Victor Habbick/Science Photo Library, 53
David Hardy/Science Photo Library, 33, 42
iStockphoto, 51, 67, 71, 74, 84

Series design and book layout:
Amy Stirnkorb

LIBRARY OF CONGRESS CATALOGING-IN-PUBLICATION DATA

Stewart, Gail B., 1949-
 UFOs / by Gail B. Stewart.
   p. cm. -- (The mysterious and unknown series)
 Includes bibliographical references and index.
 ISBN-13: 978-1-60152-030-2 (hardback)
 ISBN-10: 1-60152-030-1 (hardback)
 1. Unidentified flying objects. 2. Unidentified flying objects--Sightings and encounters. I. Title.
 TL789.S767 2007
 001.942--dc22

                                                                                    2007013351

CONTENTS

FOREWORD

"Strange is our situation here upon earth."
—*Albert Einstein*

Since the beginning of recorded history, people have been perplexed, fascinated, and even terrified by events that defy explanation. While science has demystified many of these events, such as volcanic eruptions and lunar eclipses, some continue to remain outside the scope of the provable. Do UFOs exist? Are people abducted by aliens? Can some people see into the future? These questions and many more continue to puzzle, intrigue, and confound despite the enormous advances of modern science and technology.

It is these questions, phenomena, and oddities that Reference-Point Press's *The Mysterious & Unknown* series is committed to exploring. Each volume examines historical and anecdotal evidence as well as the most recent theories surrounding the topic in debate. Fascinating primary source quotes from scientists, experts, and eyewitnesses, as well as in-depth sidebars further inform the text. Full-color illustrations and photos add to each book's visual appeal. Finally, source notes, a bibliography, and a thorough index provide further reference and research support. Whether for research or the curious reader, *The Mysterious & Unknown* series is certain to satisfy those fascinated by the unexplained.

INTRODUCTION

Not Alone

Val is a 57-year-old truck driver who lives in Edmonton, Alberta, Canada. He was driving his camper down into Montana in June 2004, when he saw something that he never expected to see. When he remembers that night he still gets goose bumps, he says. And even after almost three years, the experience of that evening is as clear and sharp as though it happened yesterday.

"I'm Just a Regular Person"

"I have to say straight up that I am not a drinking man," he says. "I don't do drugs or anything. And I'm not a person who believes in the occult or that sort of thing. I'm just a regular person. But I will say to this day that I saw a spaceship of some kind about 100 miles outside of Missoula [Montana]. It wasn't a star or a planet or something like that. It was a spacecraft—it positively could not have been anything else."

Val says that just after sunset he saw the strange object in the sky off to his left. And as he continued to drive, it got brighter and larger. "It was moving toward me," he says, "although I cannot say for certain how fast. But what I did notice was that the colors

"QUOTE"

"It's kind of hard not being able to tell people about something so sensational that happened to you. It makes you feel kind of like you're out there alone."

—A woman, who witnessed a UFO in Edmonton, Alberta, Canada in 2004.

The UFO Val saw in 2004 had many lights, much like the above image.

of the lights were the most interesting I'd seen. Bright blue—you don't see that on planes, I don't think. And as it got closer, I saw that it was five lights, not just one big one.

"I pulled over to the side of the road, because it seemed as if it was going to go right over my truck. I had the window down, because it was a very warm evening. And I noticed right away that the darned thing wasn't making any noise at all. Just gliding over.

And I could see it was huge—bigger than any plane—no, many times bigger than any plane I've ever seen. It seemed to hover overhead. And then, and I'm telling you, this is the amazing part. It just reversed its direction and took off north, over the trees."

Val says he was so amazed after the experience that he wanted to tell people about it. "I called my wife, and told her all about what happened," he says. "She knows me, and she knows I don't make things up. So she was interested in the whole experience. But she says, 'Honey, don't tell a lot of other people. You don't know what they'll say. They won't believe you.' I thought about it, and I guess she was most likely right. But it's kind of hard not being able to tell people about something so sensational that happened to you. It makes you feel kind of like you're out there alone."[1]

40 Million Americans

As unbelievable as Val's experience seemed to him, he is not at all alone in what he saw. Millions of people throughout the world have seen what they say are UFOs, or unidentified flying objects. In a national survey taken in 2002, it was found that 40 million Americans say they have seen a UFO or know someone who has.

Many sightings are like Val's—taking place in remote areas such as the plains or deserts. But there are others that occur in busy urban areas. On November 7, 2006, for example, there was a sighting at Chicago's O'Hare Airport. The UFO was dark gray, witnesses say, and well defined against the overcast sky. It had no lights but was clearly visible at 4:30 P.M. as it seemed to hover over Concourse C of the United Airlines terminal, just below the ceiling of clouds.

Twelve United employees witnessed the sighting—some pilots as well as members of the ground crew. One pilot opened the windscreen of his plane to get a better view of the object, which he estimated was about 1,500 feet (457m) above the ground. He and others watched as the object suddenly accelerated straight up through the clouds, leaving behind an open hole of blue sky in the gray blanket of cloud cover. As one witness recalled, "It was like somebody punched a hole in the sky."[2]

The witnesses are adamant that what they saw was not an aircraft or a weather balloon. They say they can recognize these better than most people because they are familiar with them. Even so they cannot say for sure what they saw.

"I tend to be scientific by nature," says one of the men, a mechanic who was in the cockpit of a Boeing 777 when he saw it. "And I don't understand why aliens would hover over a busy airport. But I know that what I saw and what a lot of other people saw stood out very clearly, and it definitely was not an [Earth] aircraft."[3]

Life-Changing Occasion

The idea of unidentified flying objects is not just an American phenomenon. Sightings have occurred all over the world in places such as Iran, Mexico, Sweden, Britain, Chile, and Kenya. In December 1999 dozens of farmers working bean fields near Beijing watched a strange object with colored lights arc through the sky in total silence. Over the next two weeks people in 12 other Chinese cities saw it, too.

And while details of sightings vary, the sense of astonishment, bewilderment, and awe seem consistent. For Val, the sighting in

Many photographs of UFOs prove to be hoaxes, like this doctored image.

Montana was, he says, "one of the things I'll never forget, not for the rest of my life."[4] A woman who experienced a sighting in

Britain in 2001 was so inspired knowing there were other worlds out there, she decided to rewrite her will, bequeathing most of her money to the poor—something she had not previously considered doing. And one of the ground crew that witnessed the sighting at O'Hare was so shaken by it, as one coworker explained, he "experienced some religious issues"[5] over it.

Stephen Gill, who investigates sightings of UFOs, says that for many who experience a sighting, the occasion is life changing. "When people see these things, it tends to shatter their self-made concept of reality."[6]

"It Sounds So *X-File*-ish"

Though millions believe that such sightings are proof of intelligent life in other places in the universe, many are reluctant to call UFOs alien spacecraft. "It sounds so *X-File*-ish," says Ali, a graduate student in physics. "It kind of conjures up images of guys sitting around with tin foil on their heads to hear alien transmissions or something." Although Ali knows that is probably not a fair representation of UFO sighters, he says he would feel embarrassed. "No matter how sure I was that's what I saw," he admits, "I think I'd be kind of reluctant to tell the world."[7]

But there are many who do report their experiences with UFOs, and some who devote thousands of hours investigating those experiences. And though many of the sightings can later be explained as something very ordinary—from a star or a reflection in a car window to a weather balloon—there are many for which there have been no ready explanations. The mystery of such cases is both perplexing and fascinating—possibly offering evidence that humans on Earth are not alone.

CHAPTER 1

Seeing Fire in the Skies

Many people are surprised to learn that UFO sightings are not limited to modern times. In fact, there have been sightings of strange objects in the sky for many centuries. Descriptions and accounts of these sightings have shown up in literature, historical records, and even painting and sculpture going back to ancient times. Some of these sightings, if they had occurred today, might have been easily explained. A meteor, for instance, could well have been perplexing to people centuries ago. However, some UFO descriptions from long ago are strikingly similar to more modern sightings.

Blazing Missiles and Flying Shields

In several Sanskrit texts of Hindu history there are references to odd, fiery sightings in the nighttime skies. In the *Dona Parva*,

This computer-generated image shows what a fleet of shiny flying saucers might look like.

for example, the author describes battles between Hindu gods in flying machines—battles that sound uncannily like modern aerial dogfights. During these battles, according to one translation, a "blazing missile possessed of the radiance of smokeless fire was discharged."[8]

In ancient accounts of the military exploits of Alexander the Great, there are descriptions of UFOs that appeared twice during his campaign in Asia and the Middle East. The first sighting in 329 B.C. occurred as Alexander and his army were crossing the river Jaxartes into India. An eyewitness described two "shining silver shields"[9] descending from the sky, diving toward the military procession, causing soldiers, horses, and elephants to panic.

Seven years later the flying shields reappeared during Alexander's siege of the city of Tyre, in what is now Lebanon. This time the shields were active participants in the battle, sending a strong beam of light through a city wall, shattering it. According to historians, Alexander's men were able to take advantage of this strange occurrence and capture the city.

Biblical UFOs?

Many ufologists (those who investigate UFO sightings) have turned their attention to the Bible as a source of unexplained sightings. For example, in the Old Testament story of the Israelites fleeing Egypt to get to the promised land, God went "before them by day in a pillar of cloud to lead them along the way, and by night in a pillar of fire to give them light, that they might travel by day and night."[10]

Equally mysterious is the vision described by the prophet Ezekiel centuries later: "As I looked, behold, a stormy wind came out of the north, and a great cloud, with brightness round about it, and fire flashing forth continually, and in the midst of the fire, as it were gleaming bronze. And from the midst of it came the likeness of four living creatures."[11] The creatures, each described as having four faces and wings, were somehow enclosed in an airborne wheel within another wheel.

Ezekiel's wheel, as the vehicle has been called, was described in detail, and that intrigued one engineer at the National Aeronautics and Space Administration (NASA). Doubtful that such a vehicle could fly given its biblical description, Josef Blumrich set about to prove it. He was astonished when he realized that it could be adapted into a workable design for a landing module launched from a larger space vehicle. The four creatures described in the Bible, said Blumrich, could have been four sets of landing apparatus, and the wings could have been helicopter blades allowing the craft to touch down gently on the ground. Blumrich later acknowledged that his project to debunk the Bible story had failed. However, he wrote, "Seldom has a total defeat been so rewarding, so fascinating, and so delightful!"[12]

The Art of UFOs

Art has proved a fascinating source of UFO speculation, too—especially biblical art. One famous example is a painting by an early Renaissance painter named Domenico Ghirlandajo. In the painting, showing Mary and the infant Jesus, there is a strange, dark, saucer-shaped object in the sky beyond Mary's left shoulder. The object is clearly of interest to a man and his dog, who are nearby. Art historians are at a loss to explain what Ghirlandajo was showing, but many ufologists believe it is a UFO.

Another painting—this one a 1350 fresco depicting the Crucifixion—shows a UFO in much more detail. The fresco, which hangs in a monastery in Kosovo, Serbia, shows a man piloting a flying vehicle—which is speeding away from the Crucifixion scene. The image, which no one has been able to explain, has caused a great deal of speculation about the presence of aliens and spaceships in biblical times.

Into the Modern Age

Such sightings and their descriptions continued to appear in each successive century from medieval times to the years of the First

World War. And while no one can say for certain when the unidentified flying objects were first seen, and by whom, experts do agree that the first modern sighting took place on June 24, 1947, by a 32-year-old Idaho businessman and pilot named Kenneth Arnold.

Arnold was piloting a small plane over the Cascade Mountains in Washington, near Mount Rainier. He and others were searching for a downed Marine Corps transport plane that was believed to have crashed a month earlier but had not yet been found. Cruising at an altitude of 9,000 feet (2743m), Arnold saw two flashes of intensely bright light and then noticed ahead of his plane a formation of nine disk-shaped objects, flying at what he realized was an incredible speed.

Arnold later tried to describe what he had seen. Their movement, he said, was "very similar to a formation of geese" or resembled "the tail of a Chinese kite that I once saw blowing in the wind" or moved "like a saucer would if you skipped it across the water." He added that "no orthodox plane would be flying like that."[13]

He opened the window to get a better look and, thinking like a pilot, tried to get an estimate of the speed of the objects. He used his cockpit clock to time one of the objects in relation to the peaks of Mount Adams and Mount Rainier, which he knew were 47 miles (75.6km) apart. His estimate put the speed of the objects in the range of 1,350 to 1,700 miles (2,173 to 2,735km) per hour. Startled, he realized this could not be possible, since no known plane of that time could get close to that speed. Even so, he could not find another estimate that made sense. He wondered if they could be some sort of guided missile being tested by the air force, but dismissed that idea, too. They banked and veered—completely unlike any missile he had ever heard of.

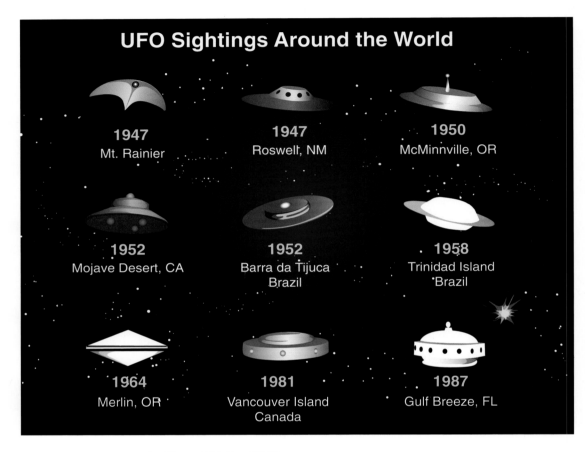

UFO Sightings Around the World

1947 Mt. Rainier	**1947** Roswell, NM	**1950** McMinnville, OR
1952 Mojave Desert, CA	**1952** Barra da Tijuca Brazil	**1958** Trinidad Island Brazil
1964 Merlin, OR	**1981** Vancouver Island Canada	**1987** Gulf Breeze, FL

A Credible Witness

When he landed Arnold told the airport manager and some other pilots about what he had seen. None could come up with an explanation. But it was an exciting story, and news of Arnold's experience quickly spread. Reporters asked Arnold again and again to repeat the story.

Although his account seemed unbelievable, Arnold impressed everyone he talked with as being a reliable, no-nonsense witness. He did not seem to be craving attention, as some did when telling a fantastic tale. He was not interested in publicity or even whether other people found his story believable. Part of his credibility lay in the fact that he was experienced with aircraft. He had been a search and rescue pilot, logging more than 4,000 hours in the air. He was also familiar with the flight conditions and geography of the Cascade Mountains. Clearly, he was someone who could be believed.

Historians say that Arnold's sighting that afternoon in 1947 was important for several reasons. As a pilot, he was definitely a knowledgeable witness. His story was also fascinating to the public, especially his comparison of the objects moving as a saucer would. Though there were some who wondered whether he had merely seen a weather phenomenon or an optical illusion, millions read about the "flying saucers," as they were dubbed by the press, and were convinced that Arnold had seen something very important.

In the next month more than 1,000 other people reported sightings, too, and because the public could not seem to get enough of such stories, the press was eager to report on every one. As UFO researcher John Spencer notes, "It seemed for a time that if your state did not have some reports of aerial visitors, your star was coming off the star-spangled banner."[14] That summer marked the beginning of the modern fascination with flying saucers—and it would continue to grow.

"A Danger to Public Calm and Safety"

Though the public seemed to have a never-ending appetite for new stories of flying saucers, the stories were frightening to many people. Those who believed that the tales were real wondered about the nature of such aliens. Did they mean harm to Earth, or were they simply gathering information? There was certainly no way to answer these questions, and it seemed that the more stories were reported, the higher the anxiety level among Americans.

As the months went by, writes one historian, government officials began to realize that "the unrelenting furor over UFOs was itself a greater danger to public calm and safety than the UFOs themselves."[15] For that reason, the government made a concerted effort to treat sighting reports with scorn or disinterest. The air force even announced late in 1947 that their own preliminary studies showed that there was nothing at all to such sightings. Military spokesmen insisted that many of the sightings were merely hoaxes or delusions, and the rest simply tricks of the eye—a pilot mistaking Venus or a meteor for a flying saucer. There was nothing to worry about, they assured the nervous public.

A Soviet Weapon?

But while the U.S. military downplayed the sightings, they were in fact carrying out their own secret investigations—for what seemed in 1947 a very good reason. While World War II had recently ended, the United States and the Soviet Union engaged in what was known as the Cold War. The spread of communism by the Soviet Union was believed to be a serious threat to the United States.

And while there was no battle being waged between the two nations, there was mutual distrust as each nation began arming itself for a future war. The U.S. Air Force, the branch of the military in charge of defending the nation's skies from enemies, wondered whether some of the UFO sightings were actually a powerful new Soviet weapon that might soon be used against the United States.

For this reason, the air force began its own investigation, carefully reviewing the most compelling of the UFO stories. By December 1947 air force officials had seen enough. They reported to the Pentagon that they found no evidence of Soviet weaponry. But they added that the phenomenon reported by Arnold "is something real and not visionary or fictitious."[16] The military urged a special ongoing investigative unit be established to collect and study every sighting from that point on.

Close Encounters of Four Different Kinds

The unit, known as Project Sign, was established on January 22, 1948. It was headed by a professor of astronomy at Northwestern University, J. Allen Hynek. Hynek's job was to sort through the boxes of files accumulated by the air force and a host of agencies and police departments throughout the United States. The government hoped that Hynek and his staff could put an end to the speculation about visitors from outer space and find rational explanations for such phenomena.

Though Hynek admitted years later that he was not a believer in the flying saucer theories, he tried to do his work with an open mind. One of the first things he did was to develop a system that allowed him to organize the sightings, as well as come up with a name for the unexplained phenomena. It was he who first called them UFOs, or unidentified flying objects. Hynek realized that the reports fell into four main types, each of which he called a "close encounter,"[17] and Hynek's classification system has remained in use to this day.

A close encounter of the first kind was the type Arnold had

"We have no evidence that they are flying saucers. Conversely, we have no evidence that they are not flying saucers. We don't know what they are."

—Air force spokesman commenting on the reported UFOs flying around Washington in 1952.

This computer-generated image shows what a UFO on the ground might look like. An occupant stands to the left of the aircraft.

experienced—a sighting of a UFO, with no physical evidence left behind. Then, as in recent years, this type made up the bulk of sighting reports—nearly 66 percent. The sighting reported by Kenneth Arnold was a close encounter of the first kind, for while he was a credible witness, he could not produce any evidence of what he saw.

Close encounters of the second kind were those in which the object left some physical traces behind. Damage to soil or foliage may occur, or in some cases witnesses have found debris they claim was left by a UFO. This type of encounter makes up about 20 percent of the reported sightings.

Encounters of the third and fourth kinds are far more rare. Those of the third kind—about 16 percent—are those in which a witness sees not only the UFO but also aliens. In close encounters of the fourth kind—only about 9 percent of cases—witnesses say they have actually had contact with aliens. Some claim to have had discussions with space visitors, and others say they have actually been abducted by them.

No Shortage of Sightings

As Project Sign—later renamed Project Blue Book—continued, Hynek and his team had no shortage of sightings to investigate. Some were easily dismissed, clearly reported by people who were only interested in publicity or whose accounts were obviously fabricated. But there were some that seemed very credible, such as a sighting reported by two members of an Eastern Airlines crew, pilot Clarence Chiles and his copilot John Whitted on July 23, 1948. Nearly six hours into their flight, they were near Montgomery, Alabama, when they saw what looked like a missile streaking directly toward their plane.

"It flashed down towards us at a terrific speed," Chiles later recalled. "We veered to the left and it passed us about 700 feet to the right."[18] The object was shaped more like a cigar than a saucer, and its surface looked metallic, although it seemed to glow blue and orange. The men estimated it to be about 30 yards (27m) long. They could see a 15-yard-long (13.7m) flame blasting out of the object's tail. And while most passengers on the plane were asleep, one passenger saw the object, too.

The investigation of the sighting found that nearly an hour before Chiles and Whitted saw the UFO, it was likely seen at the Robbins Aviation Base in Macon, Georgia. It also found that no aircraft had filed a flight plan to be in that area at that time.

Scrambling Jets to Chase UFOs

Such reports were still causing a great deal of speculation by the public. Although some of the more outlandish stories of Martians kidnapping children or flying saucers firing strange weapons at people in a Chicago suburb were viewed by nearly everyone with

"I'll Believe Them When I See Them"

In the weeks after Kenneth Arnold's famous UFO sighting in the Cascade Mountains on June 24, 1947, a flood of UFO reports followed. The U.S. Air Force received over 850 reports in a single month. One report on July 4, 1947, was that of a United Air Lines pilot named E.J. Smith. Someone asked him before a routine flight if he believed in flying saucers, and he answered, "I'll believe them when I see them." Eight minutes later, over Emmett, Idaho, Smith saw nine circular UFOs fly into view, zigzagging, merging, and splitting up before disappearing from view. His copilot and flight attendant also saw them. The objects were never identified.

Peter Brookesmith, *UFO: The Complete Sightings*. New York: Barnes and Noble, 1995, p. 46.

suspicion, sightings by experts like Chiles and Whitted were unsettling. In 1952 something happened in the nation's capital that was truly alarming—and it caused the government to decide that the topic of UFOs was officially off-limits.

On July 19, 1952, at 11:40 P.M., seven unidentified blips appeared on a radar screen at the National Airport in Washington, D.C. There was very little air traffic that night, and controllers in the tower watched, fascinated, as the blips cruised at about 120 miles (193km) per hour and then quickly left in a burst of speed. Harry Barnes, the head controller, later recalled that the blips "acted like a bunch of small kids out playing. It was helter-skelter, as if directed by some innate curiosity. At times, they moved as a group or cluster, at other times as individuals."[19]

Captain S.C. Pierman, a commercial pilot with 17 years of experience, was one of several pilots who visually confirmed what the tower was picking up on radar. Pierman later said they reminded him of shooting stars but were far too fast. "In all my years of flying," he later said, "I have seen a lot of falling or shooting stars—whatever you want to call them—but these were much faster than anything like that I have ever seen. They couldn't have been aircraft. They were moving too fast for that."[20]

When it looked as though the UFOs were flying over the restricted air space of the White House and the Capitol, Barnes notified the air force. F-94 jets were scrambled to investigate. As the jets flew over the city the objects seemed to disappear. When the jets flew back to their base the UFOs returned.

"We Don't Know What They Are"

The following Saturday the UFOs were spotted again. This time controllers checked with nearby Andrews Air Force Base and confirmed that they were seeing the same blips on their radar. Again, the air force sent fighter jets to search the skies over Washington. This time, however, one of those pilots was able to see the lights for himself. Lieutenant William Patterson tried to chase one of the objects but could not keep up. "I was at my maximum speed," he told investigators, "but . . . I ceased chasing them because I saw no chance of overtaking them."[21]

Even though the air force tried to keep the incidents secret, news leaked to reporters. Within hours, headlines throughout the nation told of flying saucers over Washington, D.C., and the military's inability to catch them. Asked for a statement, an air force spokesman explained that there was no substantive proof of what the UFOs actually were. "We have no evidence that they are flying saucers," he said. "Conversely, we have no evidence that they are not flying saucers. We don't know what they are."[22]

One investigator from Project Blue Book insisted that there was nothing to worry about. He said the blips seen by the control tower were caused by a temperature inversion, which sometimes caused false images on radar. However, this did not explain the visual verification by pilots in the air. Barnes refused to believe that a temperature inversion caused the blips he saw. "[Temperature] inversions are always recognized by experts," he said. "We are familiar with what weather conditions, flying birds, and such things can cause on radar."[23]

The Real Threat

Over the next six months the federal government cut off discussion of UFOs by insisting that it had positively verified that the radar had malfunctioned because of temperature inversions. And because the UFOs had ceased appearing over Washington, the public panic subsided. However, to prevent any future problems, a special Central Intelligence Agency (CIA) panel urged that all further sighting reports should be highly classified and that Project Blue Book should cease its investigations and concentrate on

calming the public's nervousness.

Experts say that in the following years UFO reports or sightings became more the subject of ridicule and comedy than serious science. "I remember in the late 50s how the people who said they'd seen things were viewed as odd," says Sandy, a science teacher. "They were the weird people—hermits or just a little off, you know? They were the ones portrayed on TV as people who sat around with tin foil on their heads to hear transmissions from Pluto."[24]

Government agencies soon were no longer interested in sharing information about possible UFOs. Project Blue Book explained away sightings by saying objects were not UFOs but rather stars, or Venus, or even hysteria on the part of the witness. But disinterest on the part of the government did nothing to minimize the fact that sightings continued. And many people had a lingering feeling that the government knew much more than it wanted to say.

One explanation of UFOs given is comets or shooting stars, like the comet seen here.

CHAPTER 2

UFOs and Roswell

There is no event in the history of UFO sightings that has created more controversy than that which occurred in Roswell, New Mexico, in 1947. Modern ufologists have accused the government of a massive cover-up of what they claim was the most exciting close encounter ever. The Roswell incident took place years before the panic from the Washington, D.C., sightings caused the government to stop its active investigation of UFOs. Yet many feel the government deliberately withheld crucial information in 1947 that could have proved the existence not only of UFOs but the aliens who pilot them.

An Amazing Find

The story began on the night of July 2, 1947, when a large thunderstorm moved into the area of Roswell—a town in southeastern New Mexico. A hardware dealer name Dan Wilmot and his

wife were watching the storm from their porch when they saw what they described as "a big glowing object" traveling rapidly through the sky—perhaps 500 miles (804k) per hour. The object was about 25 feet (7.6m) across and was moving southeast to northwest. Unsure of what it was, Wilmot said it looked like "two inverted saucers faced mouth to mouth."[25] They reported their sighting to the local paper, the *Roswell Daily Record*, the next day and did not think much more about it. However, in the next several days their experience would seem particularly meaningful.

The night of the storm Mac Brazel, whose sheep ranch was about 75 miles (120km) from Roswell, not only heard claps of thunder but also what sounded like an explosion. The next morning as he was checking on his sheep, he discovered that one of his fields was filled with debris from what appeared to be signs of wreckage. After looking at it more closely, he saw that it was unlike airplane debris. There were hundreds of small, dull

The Extra-terrestrial Highway was established in 1996 and runs along the eastern border of Area 51, a military base on a Nevada test site that the U.S. government has only recently admitted exists.

silver pieces of what looked like aluminum foil. On closer inspection, however, the pieces were not flimsy like foil but tough and strong. In addition, Brazel saw that there were a number of little pieces shaped like I-beams—supports used in construction. They were not made of wood or metal but of a light material that was completely unfamiliar to him.

Although the debris was odd, Brazel was unconcerned. He said later that he was used to seeing debris in his pasture, for his ranch was fairly close to both Roswell Army Air Field (RAAF) and the White Sands Missile Range. It made sense that the military might be testing a new type of aircraft. Brazel thought it was possible that if the debris belonged to some experimental plane or balloon, military officials might want to know that it crashed. He gathered up some of the pieces and a few days later gave them to the local sheriff.

"Nothing from This Earth"

Equally puzzled, the sheriff called the RAAF. Major Jesse Marcel and another intelligence officer were sent to Brazel's ranch. They found a huge, 500-foot-long (152.4m) gouge in the earth and an entire pasture littered with the debris. Marcel seemed as befuddled as Brazel and the sheriff about the wreckage. He had flight experience, and as the base intelligence officer at RAAF he was well aware of any experimental aircraft being tested—including rockets, airplanes, and balloons. He told Brazel that he had never seen such material before. He said he did not know what it was, but he did know that it was "nothing from this earth."[26]

Marcel loaded up the debris and took it to RAAF. He recalled later that he made a stop at his home to show some of the pieces to his family. Jesse Marcel Jr., 11 years old at the time, recalled that experience years later. "I can remember just like it happened yesterday, the type of material that was there," he says. "The most curious part of the debris that I saw were the I-beams, the structural members with pinkish-violet writing along the inside surface, more like geometric symbols. . . . When you see something that impressive, even as an eleven-year-old, it stays with you."[27]

The wreckage Marcel took to RAAF must have been equally impressive to the commander there, Colonel William Blanchard. After examining the debris Blanchard ordered Marcel to take it to the headquarters of the Eighth Air Force in Fort Worth, Texas. Blanchard also ordered his press secretary to issue a press release to local reporters who were calling the base with questions about the rumor of a crashed UFO.

An Astonishing Headline

The evening edition of the *Roswell Daily Record* for July 8, 1947, carried a banner headline: "RAAF Captures Flying Saucer on Ranch in Roswell Region." The article describing the find said: "The Intelligence Office of the 509th Bombardment group at Roswell Army Air Field announced at noon today that the field has come into possession of a flying saucer. . . . After the intelligence office here had inspected the instrument, it was flown to 'higher headquarters.'"[28]

That same day, ABC News featured Roswell as their lead radio story. ABC's Joe Wilson told listeners that he had learned that the saucer was being sent to Wright Field in Ohio for study. "A few moments ago," said Wilson excitedly, "I talked to officials at Wright Field who declared that they expect a so-called flying saucer to be delivered there, but it hasn't arrived as yet."[29]

News of the find reached all the way to Great Britain, where

London radio stations and newspapers reported on the events at Roswell. Because the story also included the sighting by Dan Wilmot and his wife on July 2, some readers and listeners concluded that the saucer was the same object whose remains had been found in Mac Brazel's pasture.

"Nothing to Get Excited About"

The excitement was short-lived, however. The next day General Roger Ramey did a radio interview announcing that the news about a flying saucer was untrue. He explained that the debris found in Roswell was nothing more than crushed remains of a weather balloon like those used to determine the direction and speed of high-altitude winds. It was, he insisted, "nothing to get excited about."[30] The 509th Bombardment Group had mistakenly identified the weather balloon as a flying saucer, he said.

Ramey even allowed the press to view the debris, saying it was little more than foil and balsa wood. Ramey displayed the wreckage himself while photographers took pictures, so that people could see for themselves that it was nothing at all like a flying saucer.

This seemed to end speculation about a flying saucer in Roswell. The news faded quickly from the public eye and, historians say, it would have remained that way if Jesse Marcel had not learned in 1978 that he was dying of cancer. It was then that he realized he wanted to be completely truthful about what had happened at Roswell—which was not at all like Ramey's official version. Marcel agreed to tell journalists what had happened more than 30 years before. His story led investigators to other witnesses who also agreed to come forward. In all, the researchers interviewed more than 200 witnesses or their relatives over a 16-year period.

Swapped

Marcel was interviewed by several people, including a nuclear physicist named Stanton Friedman and UFO investigators Kevin Randle and Donald Schmitt. Schmitt was director of the Center for UFO Studies (CUFOS). Agreeing to be hypnotized to allow him to recall details about his memories, Marcel told about the debris he saw in Brazel's pasture. He and others at the base who unloaded the debris were told by Ramey that they must not tell anyone what they saw. The material photographed by the press had been swapped for just what it appeared to be—aluminum foil and balsa wood. The real debris had been taken to Wright Field, where, Marcel believed, it still remained.

There was no way, Marcel said, that the wreckage of a weather balloon could have been confused with foil and balsa wood by the 509th Bombardment Group. The foil shown to the press by Ramey was certainly not the same dull silver material collected in Brazel's pasture. In one interview in 1979 Marcel talked about that material as well as one soldier's observations:

> Something that is more astounding is that the piece of metal that we brought back was so thin, just like the tinfoil in a pack of cigarette paper. I didn't pay too much attention to that at first, until one of the GIs came to me and said, "You know the metal that was in there? I tried to bend that stuff and it won't bend. I even tried it with a sledge-hammer. You can't make a dent in it."[31]

Marcel's recollection was supported by other witnesses. Brazel's oldest son, Bill, who said he had continued to find scraps of the material days after most of it was taken by the RAAF, later testified to interviewers that besides being very tough it had a peculiar characteristic that foil did not have. After folding a piece and sticking it in his pants pocket, he remembered, it would flatten out quickly with not a single wrinkle, "I had it in there, two, three days, and when I took it out and put it in the box I happened to notice that it started unfolding and flattened out. . . . I would crease it and lay it down and watch it."[32] That was certainly not true with the material shown to the press by Ramey in July 1947.

Marcel insisted the government was lying to the American public, withholding information about what had really been found at Roswell. Marcel died convinced that he had held part of a spaceship from another planet.

A Second Saucer?

As interviewers continued to talk to witnesses, they learned that the debris in Brazel's pasture was not the only wreckage found that day. A civil engineer named Grady Barnett had been working in the desert about 3 miles (5 km) from where the debris was found. Although he died in 1969—before the renewed interest in researching the Roswell incident—his neighbors came forward with information he had shared with them about that day.

Barnett told them he saw sunlight glinting off something metallic and walked toward it to investigate. He said he was joined by a team of archaeology students from the University of Pennsylvania, who were searching for Native American artifacts in the desert. They all looked at a strange craft, oval and about 30 feet (9m) across. It was split open, clearly because it had crashed in the desert. Dead bodies lay around it—bodies unlike anything

Barnett or the students had ever seen.

He later told his neighbors that the bodies had huge heads but no hair. Their eyes were oddly tiny, and they wore one-piece jumpsuits without noticeable zippers or buttons.

Within a short time, Barnett said, a U.S. Army jeep approached, and officers told Barnett and the others that the area was off limits. They were told, as Marcel had been, to keep quiet about what they had seen—that it was, Barnett recalled, "their patriotic duty."[33] Within minutes a larger group of soldiers moved in, and Barnett and the students were told to leave.

For years researchers were unable to locate any of the archaeology students to interview. Finally, however, an archaeologist came forward, saying he was one of the students in 1947 who had seen the bodies in the UFO crash. His description of the bodies was very similar to Barnett's. He too remembered being told that the area had been secured by soldiers soon after he saw the scene.

This illustration shows a UFO being struck by lightning over Roswell, New Mexico, on July 2, 1947. Some reports suggested a UFO was downed after being struck by lightning during a thunderstorm.

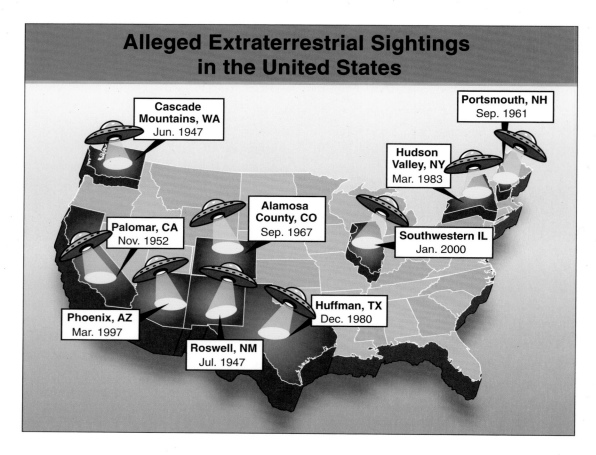

Alleged Extraterrestrial Sightings in the United States

Cascade Mountains, WA Jun. 1947

Portsmouth, NH Sep. 1961

Hudson Valley, NY Mar. 1983

Palomar, CA Nov. 1952

Alamosa County, CO Sep. 1967

Southwestern IL Jan. 2000

Phoenix, AZ Mar. 1997

Huffman, TX Dec. 1980

Roswell, NM Jul. 1947

"You're Going to Get Yourself Killed!"

The story takes a more bizarre turn with witness Glenn Dennis, who was a young mortician and part-time ambulance driver in Roswell in July 1947. In an interview conducted in 1993 Dennis told about several calls he received from RAAF on July 8, 1947, about techniques of preserving bodies and also about obtaining four child-size caskets. Although the person who called him did not give details, Dennis was curious about what was going on, and the next day he went to investigate.

He told researchers that when he got to the base infirmary, he saw a nurse that he knew. Her name was Naomi Selff. He remembered that Selff was highly agitated by his visit. She said to him, "My God, you're going to get yourself killed!"[34] Immediately, two military police officers—a redheaded officer and a black officer—wanted to know what he was doing there. Dennis explained that he had wondered if they would be needing his services They told him to leave. He recalled being threatened with harm if he returned.

Dennis said that he did not return but later called Selff. She agreed to meet with him and told him that indeed there were four dead aliens at the base. She had been present at preliminary autopsies of the bodies, two of which were badly mangled. Selff said they were about four feet tall with heads disproportionately large. She recalled that the eyes "were deeply set, the skulls were flexible, the nose was concave . . . the mouth was a fine slit, and the doctors said there was heavy cartilage instead of teeth."[35] She also said that the bodies had a strong, unpleasant odor—a fact that cut the autopsies short.

More Witnesses Come Forward

A number of witnesses came forward to tell about what had happened to the bodies after doctors at RAAF had examined them. Sergeant Melvin Brown said he was one of the men who stood guard as the crate containing the bodies was loaded onto a B-29 bomber at the base. He believed that they were being flown to Fort Worth, Texas.

This was supported by Joe Shackelford, then a lieutenant. He told interviewers he was ordered to stay at an altitude of only 8,000 feet (2,438m) for the entire flight, because the bomb bay,

The Amazing Silver Foil

O ne of the most puzzling aspects of the evidence of the UFO at Roswell was the shiny foil gathered by Jesse Marcel from Mac Brazel's ranch. Sallye Strickland Tadolini was a young girl in 1947, but she remembers vividly that Brazel's son Bill brought over a piece of the mysterious material to show her family.

"What Bill showed us was a piece of what I still think of as fabric. It was something like aluminum foil, something like satin, something like well-tanned leather in its toughness, yet it was not precisely like any one of these materials. . . . Bill passed it around and we all felt of it. I did a lot of sewing, so the feel of it made a great impression on me. It felt like no fabric I have ever touched before or since. . . . [W]hen I crumpled it in my hands, the feel was like that you notice when you crumple a leather glove in your hand. When it was released, it sprang back into its original shape. . . . I did this several times, and so did the others."

Quoted in Kevin Randle, "Roswell Explained—Again," *Fate*, September 2005, p. 12.

where the crate was held, was unpressurized, and there was a crew of military police accompanying it. From Fort Worth, say witnesses, the crate was flown to Wright Field, the same place to which the debris had been taken.

The highest-ranking military witness to come forward was Brigadier General Arthur E. Exon, who in 1947 was a lieutenant colonel at Wright Field. Many believe that his accounts of the Roswell incident and the role played by that airfield are particularly valuable. In four separate interviews in 1992 and 1993, Exon recalled flying over the Roswell area and seeing the two crash sites. Although he himself was not part of the detail that studied the bodies, he was aware that they "were all found, apparently, outside the craft itself but were in fairly good condition."[36]

Exon acknowledged that during that summer the wreckage from Roswell was examined in base laboratories, where it received "everything from chemical analysis, stress tests, compression tests, flexing. The boys who tested it said it was very unusual. They knew they had something new on their hands." Exon said flatly, "Roswell was the recovery of a craft from space."[37]

Mixed Reactions

Such new information from witnesses resulted in the publication of a raft of new books in the early 1990s. Some were highly skeptical about the stories told by these witnesses. Ufologist Karl Pflock strongly believes that UFOs have visited Earth. However, in doing his own research for his book *Roswell: Inconvenient Facts and the Will to Believe,* Pflock insists that the Roswell episode is not one of those visitations. There are simply too many inconsistencies in the stories told by witnesses that keep them from being considered hard fact.

Glenn Dennis's story has one such inconsistency. Although the former mortician claims to have been threatened by a redheaded officer and a black officer at the RAAF hospital, Pflock and others are not so sure. They point out that in 1947 the military was segregated. There were no black troops serving with white troops. There would not have been a black military police officer working alongside a white military police officer. They also wonder about Dennis's story of the nurse, Naomi Selff. To verify Dennis's story, researchers have done extensive searches for a nurse by that name but have been unsuccessful.

To many researchers, the fact that there are no records of a woman with that name ever serving as a military nurse indicates that Dennis was either wrong about her name or was fabricating the story. However, to others, such as researcher Don Schmitt, the confusion seems like more government cover-up—purging the records of Selff in order to keep the story from getting out. Said Schmitt, "Once again it appears as if they [the government] really covered their tracks."[38]

A Real Cover-Up

Even with inconsistencies in the testimonies of witnesses, the American public in the mid-1990s was asking for answers. They wondered about the Roswell crash evidence, which had been seen by so many and appeared to have been so unusual. They wondered how experts like Jesse Marcel and others could have been fooled by a simple weather balloon. It seemed as though the government was not being truthful.

In 1995, in response to public pressure, the military officially admitted that there was indeed a cover-up in 1947. However, it was not an alien spaceship that they were keeping secret but rather a top secret high-altitude spy balloon, known as Project Mogul. The balloon was actually an array of 20 to 30 balloons strung together to form a chain almost 700 feet (213m) long. Because it would fly at such a high altitude, it could spy unde-tected on the Soviet Union to verify whether their government was testing nuclear weapons. The Project Mogul aircraft was, in 1947, the largest man-made object in New Mexico at the time it was being tested.

It was, the military stated, parts of the bottom balloon in the chain which crashed to earth at Roswell. The debris of the balloon array would have indeed been more durable than foil, a fact that jibes with the story of witnesses like Marcel and Brazel. The mili-tary claimed it necessary to debunk the stories of the odd material so that word of the top secret project would not get out.

The official explanation satisfied some ufologists but not all. Some insisted that the government had lied before, and it could still be lying. Many researchers continue to stand by their work. They still maintain that aliens died at Roswell and that part of the story has not been answered by the U.S. military. If anything, the notion of a military cover-up of the second crash sight has become more believable than ever to many Americans.

"The UFO Capital of the World"

Interest in the Roswell story has continued since the revelation of Project Mogul. Each year more than 193,000 visitors come to Roswell. The town of 48,000 people, which had never been a

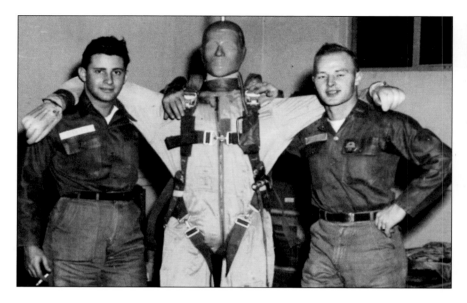

"The Roswell Report," released by the air force in 1997, was supposed to end speculation that the government covered up a UFO crash in Roswell, New Mexico in 1947. This photo from the report shows two lieutenants posing with a test dummy that was used in what the government said was a high-altitude spy balloon test.

tourist destination before, suddenly in the 1990s found itself besieged by travelers who wanted to see firsthand the place where they believe aliens crashed. In fact, the Roswell Chamber of Commerce proudly states that Roswell has become the number one tourist attraction in New Mexico. Signs outside motels proclaim that they are "Alien Friendly," and restaurants serve dishes like Cosmic Sludge, Alien Burgers, and Flying Saucer Fries.

And while some Roswell residents accept the government's version of the story, many do not. They have heard of too many people back in 1947 who were sworn to secrecy about the event by military officials. "I think something did happen," says Randhi Hesse, a Roswell business owner. "It's a historical event. There were flying saucers, as the Roswell residents call them. Were they extraterrestrial? That's the question. My great aunt said, 'It happened. End of story.' And she wouldn't say anything else about it, even to her own flesh and blood."[39]

CHAPTER 3

New Kinds of Proof

While many UFO investigators have complained about lack of cooperation by the U.S. government during the Roswell incident, others have expressed frustration over the absence of documentation of possible UFOs sightings. Evidence from witnesses is often discounted by mainstream scientists as unfounded or dismissed as inconclusive. And without evidence, UFO sightings seem to many nonbelievers to be just more crazy stories.

Where's the Proof?

Some scientists speculate that UFO sightings are not real. Surely, they say, with the thousands of sightings since Roswell, there would be some proof that an alien spaceship has actually visited this planet. However, many ufologists counter that perhaps no crash debris from an alien spaceship exists because none of the spaceships crashed.

This illustration shows a UFO flying low over choppy waters.

Hynek, who as head of Project Blue Book was once paid by the government to debunk sightings but now believes that UFOs exist, has answered that argument. Hynek agrees that the point "has come up time and time again. Why isn't there any hardware left behind? Surely they must crash sometimes, surely they must. . . . Think of the thousands of commercial planes flying daily over the U.S., yet years go by without a single crash."[40]

On the other hand, some ufologists say, there have been sightings in which witnesses have offered evidence. But skeptics routinely dismiss such evidence. Some of it entails damage to vegetation or soil where a UFO has landed. Some is photographic evidence, pictures or video taken by witnesses. Other times, the evidence is physical harm done to those who witnessed the sighting, as in a strange case on December 29, 1980.

An Encounter in Piney Woods

It was on that night at about 9:00 P.M. that 51-year-old Betty Cash was driving home on a rural highway in the Piney Woods of Texas. Along with Cash were her friend, 57-year-old Vicki Landrum, and Landrum's seven-year-old grandson Colby. The three had gone to a restaurant and were heading home. On one stretch of highway Colby noticed a bright light in the sky.

The two women looked up and were dumbstruck to see a large, brilliant object with flames shooting from the bottom. Cash quickly braked, for it seemed that the craft was going to land on the road just in front of them. They would later describe the object as metallic, with a row of bluish lights around the middle.

The inside of the car soon became intolerably hot, and the three got out. After a few moments, however, Colby was scared by the beeping and flames shooting from the craft's underbelly and ran back into the car. The two women followed him, and as they got into the car, the object elevated and flew away. The most surprising thing about the incident was that the UFO was flanked on all sides by what looked like a large flock of helicopters. "[The helicopters] seemed to rush in from all directions," Cash said later. "It seemed like they were trying to encircle the thing."[41]

Horrible Sickness

Cash recalled the three of them trying to count the helicopters, which were still in view as their car sped down the highway. They counted 23, she told investigators later, and some of them had two rotors. The women also recalled seeing a U.S. military insignia on at least one of them, and that was later backed up by a sheriff's deputy, who told investigators that he had seen a number of Chinook helicopters (which had two rotors) earlier in the evening.

By the time they returned home, they were all sick. It started with severe headaches and upset stomachs. By the next morning Cash was dangerously ill. She had what seemed like a bad sunburn over her entire body, and even her eyes were swollen shut. In the places where her skin had not been covered by clothing, she had large blisters. Colby and his grandmother were sick, too. They could not stop vomiting, and they suffered from debilitating diarrhea.

Eventually, the three were diagnosed with radiation sickness, which doctors told them could likely cause cancer in the years ahead. Their hair and fingernails soon fell out—two other symptoms of radiation sickness. Angry and confused, Cash and Landrum demanded answers. They wanted to know what had happened that night and what the UFO was. And why, they wondered, were U.S. helicopters hovering around it?

No Answers

The investigation was inconclusive. Even though other witnesses saw a bright light in the sky at the same time Cash and the Landrums did, there was no proof that satisfied investigators. Both the army and the navy used Chinook helicopters, yet nearby air bases denied that any of them had flown that night.

The burns suffered by the three witnesses are proof that *something* happened to them that night. None of the doctors who treated them could deny that exposure to intense radiation caused their symptoms. The source of the radiation, Betty Cash

insisted until she died from cancer years later, was the diamond-shaped UFO. Yet there was no proof that was solid enough for investigators. The Cash-Landrum sighting remains one of the most baffling close encounters of the second kind in modern times.

The Delphos Ring

Another incident in which a witness was physically affected occurred in the little farm town of Delphos, Kansas, on November 2, 1971. At about 7:00 P.M. young Ronnie Johnson was outside with his dog when he saw a brightly colored UFO hovering low over a field—only a few feet above the ground. He noticed that the sheep were agitated, bleating and moving as when a predator is nearby.

The boy later told investigators that he tried very hard to see details on the UFO, but because it was glowing so brilliantly, it was hard to make out any specific characteristics. He also told investigators later that he experienced blurry vision for several minutes after the sighting—perhaps, he suggested, because of the brightness of it. After his symptoms improved he ran into the house and told his parents.

They came outside in time to see the UFO rising and speeding away. His mother Emma described it as having the shape of "a giant washtub."[42] After the UFO disappeared, the family was surprised to see a strange glowing circle, approximately 8 feet (2.4m) across, on the ground directly below where Ronnie had seen the UFO. Some of the trees nearby had glowing material on them, too. In interviews with investigators the family agreed that the ground around the glow "felt strange, like a slick crust, as if the soil was crystallized."[43] Emma's fingers became numb when she touched the area.

"A Definite Maybe"?

The Johnsons called the local newspaper, the sheriff's department, and the Kansas Highway Patrol to report what they had seen. Though the ring and the trees nearby no longer glowed, it was clear that there was something different about the soil within the circle, compared with other soil in the area. They hoped authorities would see this as proof that something strange had occurred there.

The sheriff's deputy noted in his report that "we observed a ring shaped somewhat like a doughnut with a hole in the middle. The ring was completely dry . . . and outside of the ring, mud."[44] The crusty substance noticed by the family was taken to a laboratory for analysis. The material was found to be a plant, somewhere between a fungus and a type of bacteria. It is known to fluoresce, or glow, under certain circumstances, according to authorities.

"Was that proof that a UFO had been there? Not really," says astronomy student Mark Davidson, who says he has always been interested in the case. "It raised as many questions as it answered. But there was no evidence that the Johnson family had tried to pull off a hoax of any sort. The Delphos Ring, as the incident is called, is still considered an unexplainable sighting. In other words, the proof offered was not good enough to nail it as a UFO. It's what some [UFO] believers call a 'definite maybe.'"[45]

A Sighting in France

The Delphos Ring is not the only UFO sighting in which an obvious physical change occurred to nearby soil and vegetation. On January 8, 1981, a retired technician in Trans-en-Provence in the south of France, was working outside in his garden in the

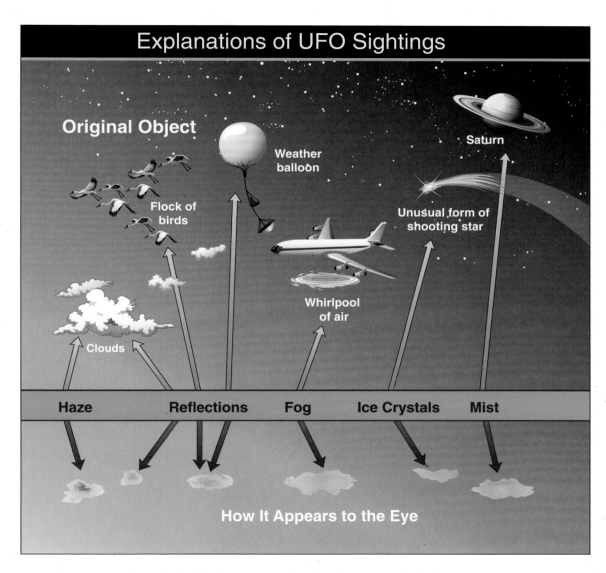

Explanations of UFO Sightings

Original Object

Flock of birds

Weather balloon

Saturn

Unusual form of shooting star

Whirlpool of air

Clouds

| Haze | Reflections | Fog | Ice Crystals | Mist |

How It Appears to the Eye

late afternoon when he heard an unusual whistling sound. As he turned, he saw a flying device descending onto the grass on the edge of his property.

The man, 55-year-old Renato Nicolai, moved toward the device to get a closer look. He later told investigators that it was the color of lead and the shape of two inverted saucers, one on top of the other. He estimated that the UFO was about 4 feet (1.2m) high and had two small circular projections underneath it, which he guessed might have been landing gear. "The device," he said later, "which was not spinning, was coming lower toward the ground. I was only hearing a slight whistling sound. I was not seeing any flames below or around the device."[46]

The device landed, he said, and then quickly lifted off again, still whistling. After the UFO ascended, Nicolai walked closer to the area where it had landed. He saw two circles, one inside the other, on the ground. One was about 7.2 feet (2.2m) in diameter, the other slightly larger, measuring about 7.9 feet (2.4m) in diameter. He reported his experience to the police, who examined and documented the circles.

Young Plants That Turned Old

The incident was reported to a scientist at the National French Center for Space Studies, a government agency that investigates sightings of UFOs by its citizens. The scientist, Jean-Jacques Velasco, first determined that no military aircraft had been in the vicinity on that day. He also took samples of soil and wild alfalfa (the vegetation growing in Nicolai's back yard) from within the ring area, as well as control samples from outside it, and submitted them to rigorous testing in a laboratory.

What technicians found was stunning. First, the soil within the ring showed that it had been subjected to heavy mechanical pressure, and soon afterward had withstood powerful heating up to 600°F (315.6°C). The alfalfa also showed significant change

within the ring. Its chlorophyll, the green substance in the plant that helps it turn sunlight into energy, was weakened from 30 to 50 percent.

The young leaves were especially odd—it appeared that they had aged significantly. In other words, the lead scientist in the case explained, "[the young leaves] had all the characteristics of their age, but they presented the biochemical characteristics of an advanced age: old leaves! And that does not resemble anything that we know on our planet."[47]

This case did not provide definitive proof that a UFO was responsible for the changes. However, experts stated, it was impossible to ignore that something unusual and unexplainable had occurred in Nicolai's backyard. "We cannot give a precise and unique interpretation to this remarkable combination of

Many UFO sightings are reported in remote desert areas, such as this one in Arizona.

results," the final report stated. "We can state that there is, none-theless, another confirmation of a very significant event which happened on this spot."[48]

Crop Circles as UFO Evidence

Pressure on the soil and marked change in vegetation has also been noted in a phenomenon called crop circles, too. Crop circles are large-scale designs made in farm fields by the depression of plants. Reports of these circles go as far back as the seventeenth century, and they are as mysterious in modern times as they were then. Crop circles have frequently been linked to UFOs because they often appear after sightings of unidentified spacecraft or large orange balls of light in the sky.

The most frequent design is a circle, although some crop cir-cles are far more intricate. As of July 2006 over 10,000 have been reported in 70 countries around the world, including the United States, Russia, Canada, Brazil, and South Africa—but the major-ity are found in Britain. They appear most often in fields of barley and wheat, but crop circles have been documented in fields of rice and corn—and the designs have even been seen in sand and snow. There are no footprints or tracks leading to or from the de-signs. The images can be seen from hilltops and mountains, but are best viewed from airplanes—a fact that ufologists say makes UFO involvement more likely.

They are most often created at night, especially on the short-est nights of the year in midsummer. Many people have camped out in fields on these nights, hoping to get a glimpse of whatever is responsible for them, but thus far have not been successful. The fact that the designs seem to be created very quickly may make their discovery that much more difficult. In some cases,

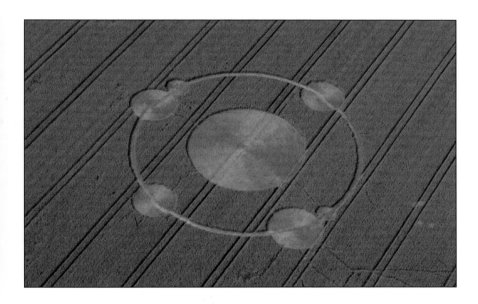

Crop circles, like this one found in Slovenia, are sometimes linked to UFOs because they often appear after sightings of unidentified spacecraft or other unexplained activity.

crop circles have been made in a matter of minutes. In 1996 a pilot flying over the large Stonehenge monument in the south of England was stunned to see a massive design where none had existed during a flyover 45 minutes earlier. According to crop circle researcher Freddy Silva, this "huge 900-foot formation, comprising 149 meticulously layered circles . . . lay beside the heavily-patrolled monument." So large and intricate was it, says Silva, that "it took a team of eleven—including myself—no less than five hours just to survey the formation."[49]

Hoaxes?

Some people believe that all crop circles are being construct-ed as hoaxes. They feel that the confessions of two 60-year-old Englishmen, David Chorley and Douglas Bower, are proof. Chor-ley and Bower came forward in 1981 and said they had been fak-ing crop circles throughout England for many years. They told

As of July 2006
over 10,000 crop
circles have been
reported in 70
countries around the
world, including the
United States, Russia,
Canada, Brazil, and
South Africa—but the
majority are found
in Britain.

investigators how they did it, demonstrating a system of long wooden boards and rope to depress the plants without leaving telltale footprints.

However, it became clear to the investigators in Britain that the two men were claiming responsibility for things they had not really done. Writes Freddy Silva, "When confronted to provide evidence on certain claimed formations, Doug and Dave changed their story, even reversing previous claims; or they simply could not explain unusual features found in the genuine phenomenon."[50] These unusual features, by which real crop circles differ from those created by Chorley and Bower (and other copycats), are the physiological effects on the vegetation and the soil in such circles. These effects would be virtually impossible to mimic.

Changes in Soil and Vegetation

One characteristic of true crop circles is the change in the soil. Scientists have identified radioactive elements in the soil within a new crop circle—elements which last only three or four hours before dissipating. They also say that the soil is much harder than that outside of a crop circle, possibly because of some intense pressure on it.

The plants themselves are not crushed or trampled, but rather bent about an inch off the ground in a manner that does not break or damage the plant's stem. Biophysicists have discovered that plants in a crop circle are actually subjected to an instantaneous surge of intense heat, which softens the stems so that they bend at the same 90 degree angle. Once they bend, the stems then harden into that new shape. No one knows how this is accomplished. Biophysicists have proposed that the burst of heat

would likely be from a source of microwave or infrasound, although they are baffled as to what that source might be. There are no breaks or other damage to the stems, and every seed in the plant remains intact. The plants can continue to grow in their new shape.

In addition to these changes in the plants and soil within a crop circle, the designs themselves have convinced some ufologists that the circles were created by intelligent extraterrestrial life. Perhaps alien beings are trying to communicate what they understand about life on Earth or to provide information about their own planet. For example, some designs appear to be extremely complex, such as one in the south of England that shows

Mutilations on a Montana Ranch

Montana rancher John Peterson spotted one of his healthy young cows mysteriously mutilated in November 2006. The cow had been dissected with stunning precision. The left side of her face was carved off, and the exposed bones were as clean as if they had been boiled.

Peterson has seen predator-killed cattle, but is certain this was not one of them. There were no footprints, no blood spills, and no sign of any struggle. Another mysterious aspect of the case is that the carcass was not eaten by birds, coyotes, or other hungry scavengers. That is very unusual, for there are many species of animals that live off dead animals.

One clue was that there was an impression in the field, as if the cow had lain down. But there were no footprints leading to where the cow was found and no drag marks. It was, writes reporter Karen Ogden, "as if the bovine had fallen from the sky—and bounced."

Karen Ogden, "Cattle Mutilation Stuns Ranchers," *Great Falls* (MT) *Tribune*, November 12, 2006.

the double helix of the DNA molecule, or another that appears to be an astronomy map, depicting various planets and moons in a much different solar system than our own.

The Slaughter of Animals

A final phenomenon that has been linked to UFOs is the very strange killing of animals—especially cattle—in areas where there has been an increase in UFO sightings. One of the first reported animal mutilations occurred in 1967, when a woman in Alamosa County, Colorado, discovered that her pony Lady had been mysteriously killed. But the killing was eerily unlike anything law enforcement officials had ever seen. The characteristics of this killing had the characteristics found in most animal mutilations that have occurred since.

The pony's flesh had been carved away from the bones with what was described as surgical precision. Its organs were removed but were absent from the scene. Puzzling to investigators was the lack of blood. In a killing which should have produced gallons of blood spilled on the ground, there was virtually none. Equally mysterious was the lack of footprints near the carcass—incredibly, not even hoofprints from the pony.

The connection with UFOs was made by area residents. In the days before the discovery of the mutilation, several UFO sightings had taken place. And with an inexplicable, savage killing of a pony following the sightings, many residents of Alamosa County wondered if aliens might have been responsible. And, some wondered, might the lack of prints around the pony and the lack of blood at the scene mean that the animal was killed elsewhere, and later dumped from the UFO?

No Answers

Since Lady's mysterious death, hundreds of other animals—usually cattle or horses—have met the same fate. And the mutilations were not only occurring in the United States but also in Mexico and other places in Central and South America.

In Argentina UFO sightings have been reported just before mutilated animals were discovered. One rancher from the San Luis province was returning home one evening and saw three slow-moving saucer-shaped objects emitting a loud buzzing noise as they lit the ground below them. Not long afterward three mutilated cattle were discovered. A veterinarian who examined the bodies said that the incisions were made by "some sort of heating element."[51] And like the victims in the United States, these cattle had been drained of blood.

Daniel Belot, a veterinarian who examined many of the mutilated cattle in Argentina had no more answers than his counterparts in the United States. "Those who haven't seen [the mutilations] cannot understand the magnitude of the situation," he said. "The facts occurred, they are very strange and cannot be disputed, but I don't know what to attribute them to. I wouldn't want to chance it."[52]

Whether the animal deaths in the United States, Argentina, and other places have anything to do with the UFOs researchers cannot say for sure. But the bloodless carcasses are yet another mystery in the search for proof of visitors from elsewhere in the universe.

CHAPTER 4

Alien Abductions

Many people have a hard time believing UFOs have visited Earth even with accounts of sightings from around the world. But no encounter with a UFO is harder to accept than an encounter of the fourth kind. This is the type in which a person has actual contact with alien beings—even, as some claim, being taken against their will.

Lost Minutes in a Police Log

One man who had such an experience is Herbert Schirmer, who in 1967 was an Ashland, Nebraska, police officer. That was the year that he had a well-publicized encounter with a UFO and the aliens on board that craft. Though his story was difficult for others to believe, he has never wavered from his account of the encounter.

It began on the evening of December 3, 1967, when Schirmer came to an abrupt stop in front of a large, football-shaped object

Some people who claim to have been abducted report that a powerful beam of light pulls them into the waiting spacecraft.

that was hovering about eight feet above the road. He watched as it rose higher and sped away. When he returned to the station, he noted in his shift report that he had seen a flying saucer but took no further action. However, from the time that he saw the UFO until the next day, Schirmer did not feel well. He had a buzzing sound in his ears and a painful headache. In addition, he had a strange two-inch-long red welt on the back of his neck—a mark that he could not explain.

Because Schirmer was a reliable, honest police officer, his report was passed on to the Condon Committee, the government investigative group that looked into UFO sightings for a brief time in the 1960s. Schirmer took and passed a lie detector test. However, members of the Condon Committee were concerned about a discrepancy in the police officer's original report. Schirmer could not account for about 20 minutes in his time log. He could not remember what had occurred between the time he witnessed the UFO and headed back to the station. To find out what had happened, the committee asked Schirmer to be hypnotized. Maybe, they hoped, his memory would improve under hypnosis.

"Are You the Watchman of This Town?"

The story told by the police officer was astonishing. He said that the UFO had landed directly in front of his squad car, and almost immediately a hatch opened. It was then, he said, that he came face to face with an alien:

> [A] shape of a man came out and walked over to the front of the patrol car. Then a second man came out of the craft and walked over to the car. The first man stood in front of the patrol car and, holding a small box-like object pressed something. A green mist came out, spraying all over the patrol car. The other man walked over to the driver's side of the car and reaching inside, pressed a silver object against my neck, directly under my left ear. I felt a tingling sensation go through my whole body.[53]

Schirmer said one of the aliens asked him, "Are you the watchman of this town?"[54] When he answered that yes, he was, the alien took him to the UFO, where he climbed up a ladder to enter the craft. The alien explained how the craft operated and showed him the instrument panels and computers. He learned, too, that the spaceship had come to recharge its energy supplies by bleeding electricity from power lines.

The encounter lasted approximately 20 minutes, which would account for the lost time in the police log. The red mark later noticed on his neck was also explained by the silver object the alien had pressed to his neck, although other than the tingling sensation, he was unclear about the purpose of the object.

Schirmer's encounter was one of the few taken seriously by the Condon Committee, almost solely because of his standing as a police officer. Even so, the lack of evidence that he met with aliens or even that a UFO landed on that Nebraska highway resulted in the case being officially closed.

The Hills

The gap of missing time experienced by Schirmer is a common part of other alien encounter stories, too. Sometimes the gap is a few minutes, other times much longer. Betty and Barney Hill, a New Hampshire couple, found that between seeing unusual lights in the sky and returning to their home, they had more than two hours of time unaccounted for. And as with Schirmer, hypnosis enabled them to provide details of what had occurred during that time.

The experience began on September 19, 1961, when the Hills were driving home to New Hampshire from a short vacation. Betty noticed a rapidly moving light in the sky, and it soon seemed to them that the lights were following their car. Barney stopped the car so that they could get a better look. As he pulled the car to the shoulder, the saucer-shaped UFO circled around, hovering to the right of them about 100 feet (30.4m) off the ground.

Barney used binoculars to view what clearly was neither a plane nor a satellite. He later remembered seeing portholes in the side of the craft, and behind those portholes he could see a group of humanlike figures with shiny black uniforms. Betty, still sitting in the car, could hear her husband screaming, "I don't believe it! I don't believe it!"[55] Terrified, Barney ran back to the car and drove off as quickly as he could, hoping to escape what appeared to be the greatest danger they had ever faced.

Missing Time and Other Questions

They reached home and felt that they were safe. However, they realized that somehow two hours of their evening was unaccounted for. Comparing memories, neither could recall a 35-mile (56km) stretch of road that they had to have driven. They remembered seeing the lights of the UFO. And after that, nothing.

In addition to their frustration about their limited memories, both Betty and Barney were having trouble with stress. Betty was having vivid nightmares about UFOs and aliens standing in the middle of a highway, not allowing the Hills to pass. In her dreams she and Barney were forced onto a space ship and made to undergo physical examinations. Barney did not have nightmares but instead developed ulcers and panic attacks, during which he was afraid to leave the house. He felt that these health issues were the result of the UFO sighting and agreed with Betty that there must be something more that occurred that night—something that they were not able to remember.

In December 1963 Barney's physician referred them both to Boston psychiatrist Benjamin Simon. Simon believed that hypnosis could help the couple recall details about their UFO

sighting that would alleviate their stress. Even though the sessions with Simon began more than two years after their UFO experience, under hypnosis both husband and wife were able to recall the night in amazing detail.

"I Could Feel Them Touching My Skin"

It became apparent that many of Betty's nightmares were grounded in real events of that night in 1961. Under hypnosis she gave a detailed description of being led into the UFO by aliens and ushered into a large examination room:

> I go into this room and some of the men come in the room with this man who speaks English. They stay a minute—I don't know who they are; I guess maybe they're the crew . . . and another man comes in. I haven't seen him before. I think he's a doctor. They bring the machine over . . . it's something like a microscope, only a microscope with a big lens. I had an idea they were taking pictures of my skin.[56]

Betty recalled that aliens took samples of her skin, fingernails, hair, and even the wax in her ears. She also remembered a painful test in which one of the examiners stuck a long needle in her navel. She told him that it was very painful. "I'm telling him, 'It's hurting, it's hurting, take it out, take it out!'" Betty recalled. "And the leader comes over and he puts his hand, rubs his hand in front of my eyes, and he says it will be all right. . . . And all the pain goes away."[57]

Barney, too, remembered details about the experience he had

not been able to recall earlier. He was led into an examination room different from the one that his wife was in:

> I could feel them examining me with their hands. . . . They looked at my back, and I could feel them touching my skin . . . , as if they were counting [the vertebrae in] my spinal column . . . and then I was turned over, and again I was looked at. My mouth was opened and I could feel two fingers pulling it back. Then I heard as if some more men came in, and I could feel them rustling around on the left side of the table. . . . Something scratched very lightly, like a stick against my left arm. And then those men left.[58]

No Souvenirs?

Simon believed that the Hills were convinced that aliens had abducted them. However, he felt that their experience was imaginary. Simon theorized that stress from the original sighting of a UFO—or whatever it might have been—left the Hills confused and frightened. Those emotions likely caused the Hills to transfer Betty's nightmares into what they thought to be real experiences.

Though the Hills continued to insist that their abduction was real, most of the scientific community rejected their claim. The reason for the skepticism was lack of proof. UFO skeptic and debunker Philip Klass wonders why not a single person who claims to have been abducted "ever returned from his or her travels bearing the alien equivalent of an ashtray or matchbook."[59]

Some ufologists who believe that the abduction stories are

true disagree with Klass, saying that there have indeed been such "souvenirs." For example, Betty Hill recalled the aliens showing her a star map. After one of her hypnosis sessions she was able to draw the map. Amateur astronomer Margaret Fish decided to investigate whether that map could align with any known astronomy maps. Fish built a scale model of the known stars within a radius of 33 light years from Earth based on the 1969 text *Catalogue of Nearby Stars.* Hill's map closely matched a view of Earth's sun from a nearby star system called Zeta Reticula. However, most astronomers scoffed at Fish's finding, saying the resemblance was just a lucky coincidence—that Hill's crudely drawn map was hardly proof of an alien abduction.

Alien Implants

Others have pointed to scars or other unexplained marks on an alleged abductee's body—such as the long welt on Schirmer's neck—as physical proof that they had an encounter with aliens. However, skeptics say there is no way of knowing how a person got such a mark or whether it was caused by an alien.

Of more interest are objects that are found embedded under the skin—either felt by an abductee sometime after the experience or noticed on an X-ray by a doctor. Some people who say they have been abducted recall under hypnosis that the object was placed there by an alien during a physical examination.

Ray, a 35-year-old San Francisco man who claimed to have been abducted in 1991, found three hard, round bumps under his skin. One appeared under the skin of his armpit, another under his scalp, and a third was found in an X-ray of his sinus cavity. Doctors examined them and pronounced them to be cysts, which sometimes form naturally in the body. However, Ray said they could not be cysts, because he recalled an alien telling him they were important. Ray said he was told by the aliens who abducted him that one of the devices was a tracking device, and the other two were supposed to monitor his breathing and his dreaming. Although he was aware his doctors did not believe him, Ray insisted that they had been placed in his body during his abduction.

While many doctors find such explanations impossible to believe, a few have been willing to entertain the idea that such objects may be just what the abductees claim they are. One is California podiatrist Roger Leir, who has operated on a number of patients who claim that they have had devices implanted in their bodies. In 1995 he removed a small whitish ball from the soft tissue of an abductee's leg. Analysis of the object showed it contained a number of metals, which Leir believes could very well mean that it was an implant from her UFO experience. "I am not a UFO nut," he explained. "I'm a doctor, a skeptical man of science. But until someone can prove otherwise, I have to work on the assumption that these implants are of alien origin."[60]

"Little Nobodies"

Some ufologists estimate that only about 1,000 people have had experiences of being abducted by aliens. Others think the number may be higher and that some abductees do not remember the event or are too afraid to tell other people about it.

Those who say they have had a close encounter of the fourth kind know that others may view them as crazy. UFO skeptics often say that claims of abduction by aliens are an attention-getting device or the ravings of alcoholics or drug users. Klass has referred to people who make such claims as "little nobodies who want to be on TV."[61]

Abductees bristle at the idea that they would make up alien abduction experiences. Why would anyone invent such stories, they ask, when the results are so negative? Besides suffering a number of physical problems after the abduction, such as stress and panic disorders, many have lost their jobs because employers or coworkers deem them unbalanced. One man, interviewed by anchorman Peter Jennings in an ABC News special, said he was abducted by four aliens who took him from his own bedroom. He says that even years after the event he cannot talk about his experience without crying.

"Perfectly Ordinary People"

Schirmer, the police officer whose UFO experience was well publicized when the Condon committee investigated it, suffered, too. He became a pariah in his hometown—his car was vandalized, and even when he made a traffic stop he was not taken seriously. "I would give somebody a traffic ticket," he says, "and they would look at me and laugh, and tear up the ticket. What could I do?"[62] He did not last long as a police officer after that. Though he tried getting work in other cities, word eventually reached his new employers about his UFO experience, and he was asked to resign.

A scriptwriter named Jill lost her job, too. She says she made the mistake of confiding to coworkers about her abduction experience. Soon afterward she was fired. The experience and its aftermath have made her life stressful, difficult, and—because she cannot talk about it with others—incredibly lonely. "All [abductees] want," she says, "is to be treated like normal, intelligent adults."[63]

Another abductee agrees, saying that it may surprise people to find out that she and other abductees are quite average, everyday citizens. "We're perfectly ordinary people," she says. "We're probably your co-workers, your family, or your friends, and we're having quite extraordinary experiences, and we're all trying to find out what's happening to us."[64]

This illustration shows a commonly described alien with large eyes, grayish skin, and a slender body.

The Problem with Hypnosis

Some abductees point to the fact that many of them have passed lie detector tests. But psychologists say that passing a lie detector test is not proof that the event was real. "That doesn't mean that the person taking the test was really abducted by aliens," says Jeanne, a Rochester, Minnesota, psychologist. "Passing a lie detector doesn't mean that. What it does mean is that the person is answering the questions [on the lie detector test] truthfully—as far as he or she knows."[65]

Some experts believe that the process of hypnosis is responsible for people believing that they were abducted. In fact, many psychiatrists believe it is irresponsible to use hypnosis for abduction cases, for the people are vulnerable and often frightened. When a person is in that mental state, they say, it is easy for a well-meaning hypnotist to plant false memories.

"We've seen that problem over and over in some sexual abuse cases," says Lynn, a family psychologist. "Subjects recall instances of abuse, especially from many years before, that never really happened. It isn't the fault of the person being hypnotized, but [has] everything to do with the hypnotist. You can't believe what the tiniest suggestion on the part of the hypnotist can lead to."[66]

In a 2002 University of California study researchers found how far-reaching the effects of a planted memory are. In one experiment, for example, they wanted to find out how much people could remember about a past trip to Disneyland and suggested to their subjects that they might have seen Bugs Bunny (who is not a Disney character) there. Interestingly, 36 percent of those subjects agreed that they had seen him and had even shaken his hand.

When dealing with a repressed, or buried, memory, the same thing could easily happen with an overeager hypnotist. "If the

"I Was Five Years Old"

Most abductees who report their experiences are adults, but some experts say it is not uncommon for children to be taken. They do not always share their experience—either because they have not got the vocabulary or perhaps because they are not sure whether they will be believed. One woman recalled being abducted from her bed as a little girl:

"I was five years old . . . [I] awakened for some reason to see seven strange looking forms at the foot of my bed—approximately four feet tall, large black eyes round shaped, grayish white skin, large head, very thin body, long arms, fingers, and toes. They then seemed to raise me out of the bed without touching me and stayed below up the stairs and outside. There was a very bright light coming down from the sky which seemed to draw us up into it. Next thing I saw was being in a room lying on a table with these beings around me again."

Quoted in David Jacobs, *Secret Life: Firsthand Documented Accounts of UFO Abductions.* New York: Simon & Schuster, 1992, p. 248.

hypnotist is a big believer in UFOs, that could easily shade the way questions are phrased," says Lynn. "It may not be intentional on the part of the hypnotist, but the results are often unreliable, all the same."[67]

Only a Dream?

Many experts believe, too, that a particular sleep disorder called sleep paralysis may explain people's memories of alien abduction. This occurs during a stage of sleep called REM (short for "rapid eye movement") sleep. REM sleep is the stage in which people experience dreams. During this stage the body actually turns itself off, disconnecting from the brain. This, experts know, is a safety feature that keeps people from acting out their dreams while they are sleeping—and in the process hurt themselves or others.

But in a small percentage of the population, there is a disturbance in the transition from REM sleep and waking. For a short time their bodies are still in REM sleep—momentarily paralyzed—but their brains are semi-awake. After a moment the body catches up, but in the meantime they may be experiencing the terrifying sensation of having vivid dreams while awake and not being unable to move a muscle.

Harvard psychologist Richard McNally did a study of 10 adults in 2003 who claimed that they had been abducted by aliens. Interestingly, all of them had had episodes of sleep paralysis, and all said that prior to the abduction they were open to the idea that aliens and UFOs were real. Some had had hallucinations during episodes of sleep paralysis before the abduction. And McNally found that after they were abducted, eight of them turned to hypnotists to help them discover details about what had happened to them.

This illustration shows a frightening encounter with aliens. Some skeptics believe that alien encounters are nothing more than vivid nightmares.

McNally's belief was that the abductees were not consciously making up their remarkable stories. Instead, he concluded that the abduction stories resulted from a combination of several factors. "When you piece together the New Age beliefs [in UFOs], the hallucinations, the fantasy proneness and get a little help from the memory recovery folks," he says, "you have yourself an alien abduction."[68]

"These People Have Actually Experienced Something"

But there are many who reject the idea of a sleep disorder being responsible for their experience. "It's not some vague apparition or something," protests one abductee. "These guys were three-dimensionally in the room with me."[69] Others say the sleep disorder does not explain experiences of people being taken from their homes and cars while awake.

The late John Mack, a Harvard psychiatry professor who did landmark work with hypnosis and abductees, wholeheartedly believed that the experiences he heard about from his patients were real. Though he originally began the study as a skeptic, he admitted to becoming a believer as he heard story after story that coincided with UFO sightings. He saw distinctive cuts and marks on the skin of victims. And most of all, he was moved by their stories. Whether young children, middle-aged people, or the elderly, their experiences were very similar. Mack declared, "You have the sense that these people have actually experienced something of great meaning and depth and profundity."[70]

CHAPTER 5

"I Say, Let this Investigation Begin"

Each year the number of eyewitness accounts of UFOs continues to grow. But many experts say that we are actually no closer to understanding UFOs than our ancestors were centuries ago. That fact is frustrating to many who have witnessed UFOs and who are eager to learn more about what they saw.

"That's Kind of Sad, I Think"

"I think it's particularly bad news," says Lorraine, who saw a UFO while camping in the Boundary Waters of Minnesota two years ago.

> One of the things my husband and I have talked about [since the sighting] is what an amazing time it is to be alive—so much technology and science, and new things being discovered and invented

This small, round cloud could be mistaken for a UFO when moonlight and water reflect different shapes and colors to the observer.

all the time. And yet, here is this gigantic, bright thing, all lit up in blue and red, just gliding over our heads, and no one really knows what it is. And in a way, the fact that it's a mystery is kind of neat. Like there is still something unknown out there to puzzle over.

Lorraine says she and Dennis, her husband, have talked a lot about the possibilities. "Maybe it was a space traveler," she says.

Maybe it's some strange new type of comet or astronomy thing that no one ever suspected was out there, and it just happened to cruise right over me and Dennis. I mean, who knows, right? We'd tell each other that we're pretty young yet—both of us are 32, and we figure in our lifetime, scientists will figure it out.

But the truth is, it appears that nobody is even interested in this mystery. I mean, not only don't scientists or the government or the military know what these are—they don't even believe people like me and Dennis, who have seen one! So with disinterest on the part of the scientists, I guess I figure that there isn't much chance of our ever finding out what it was. And that's kind of sad, I think.[71]

No Further Investigations Warranted

The basis of the problem is that the scientific community in the United States is no longer investigating UFO sightings. There is no longer a single government agency that encourages Americans to report strange sightings. Project Blue Book ended in the late 1960s. In 1967 President Gerald Ford asked physicist Edward Condon to assemble a committee of scientists to decide whether or not there was any point in continuing governmental UFO investigations.

The committee selected 56 cases from the thousands reported to Project Blue Book and found that none of them contained any evidence of alien beings or UFOs. Their recommendation was that such investigations were unwarranted:

The existence of either alien flying vehicles or unknown natural phenomena is not indicated by the evidence we have examined. We are left with no artifact of alien cultures, no direct or indirect

Did You Know?

France is the only nation that has tackled serious UFO research.

evidence of anything extraordinary, few [if any] pictures that cannot be shown to be fake . . . and many examples of impressive reports which lost their strangeness as their claims were investigated.[72]

The committee's findings were the object of a great deal of criticism for their choice of cases to review. Ufologist Peter Davenport notes that the committee chose cases that were relatively weak to begin with. "When one looks at the cases the Condon Commission settled on for investigation to the exclusion of other more dramatic cases," he said, "a reasonable person would come to the conclusion that these people did not want to get to the bottom of the phenomenon."[73]

An Uneasy Relationship

As a result of the committee's work, the government decided that it no longer needed to be in the UFO business. No government agency, no branch of the military, nor any other department in federal, state, or local government would investigate UFO sightings. Any investigations would be left to small, private scientific groups with limited budgets.

Some scientists worry that this development is a step in the wrong direction. They say that the disinterest in UFOs on the part of the government has caused an uneasy relationship between these small independent groups and the larger scientific community, especially those scientists who work in well-funded government agencies. They point out that through the centuries, mainstream science has dismissed or ridiculed many things that have later been proven real—meteors, a round Earth, and gravity, to name a few.

Peter Sturrock, professor of applied physics at Stanford University, believes that even if the official position of the scientific community is that UFOs do not exist, scientists should still try to find out what people are actually seeing. "The real problem has been that scientists have tended to say, 'UFOs mean extraterrestrials, there can't be extraterrestrials, therefore, we can forget UFO reports,'" Sturrock says. "We say, 'Forget the theories about what caused the evidence. Look at the evidence and see what it has to tell us.'"[74]

Getting Rid of the Laugh Factor

Sturrock and others have suggested that mainstream science needs to take another look at unexplained phenomena such as UFOs. By applying the scientific method to the study—gathering and testing evidence, looking at a range of possibilities, and not being too quick to formulate a conclusion—it might be possible to get real answers about what people have been seeing for centuries. The answers may have nothing at all to do with aliens and outer space but instead be natural phenomena that are not yet understood. Says Sturrock, "We've been getting UFO reports worldwide for fifty years that we've been ignoring for fifty years. Let's not ignore them for another fifty years."[75]

Sturrock points out that France is the only nation that has tackled serious UFO research. It has set up an agency that deals with the collection of UFO evidence in much the same way forensic data at a crime scene is gathered. The government offers modest financial help to university laboratories to study evidence, too. Using this system, scientists can be certain that there is a reliable chain of evidence that makes it less likely for someone to fabricate a story.

Most important, it would be crucial to eliminate what some ufologists term "the laugh factor"—the automatic permission society gives itself to ridicule anyone who claims to have seen a UFO or who claims to have been abducted by aliens. When people are sure that they will be mocked, they are less likely to report or even talk about something they have seen—something that might very well be a case that could prove the existence of a UFO.

"A Big House Floating in the Air"

Many ufologists have suggested that scientists should revisit some of the most interesting cases of UFO sightings. Such sightings could be singled out because of compelling evidence or perhaps because of the quality of the witnesses. One case that has intrigued many in recent years is one in which no physical evidence was found. The witnessses in this case included five police officers; their training as careful observers made them compelling witnesses.

The sighting, which took place in the early morning hours of January 5, 2000, involved a huge, triangular UFO. It was seen first by a 66-year-old miniature golf course owner named Melvern Noll. He had just stepped out of his pickup truck to check the pipes in the golf course office. He wanted to make sure they had not frozen. While there, he saw what he first thought was a big star very low in the northeastern sky. Noll said he did not think much about it until he came back outside a few minutes later. It was then he realized that it was not a star.

"I looked up and there it was," he says, "just like a big house floating in the air, with windows in it and a bright light on the inside, like there might've been a big room in there." He was not certain how big it was, but told police that he thought it was at least the size of a football field. He recalls that the object was moving very slowly, perhaps 50 miles (80km) per hour, about 800 feet (243m) above him, providing a clear view of its side and bottom. "I just couldn't believe my eyes what I was seeing up there," he says. "I mean, there was no noise, nothing! And I was looking for wings, and I couldn't see no wings on it. I thought, 'What the heck is it?'"[76]

"Zero Noise"

Noll drove to the nearby Highland, Illinois, police station and told them what he had seen. The dispatcher put out a call to officers to watch for a UFO—which resulted in scoffing and laughter over the radio. But the laughter quickly changed to astonishment for Officer Ed Barton when he, too, spotted the UFO. He noticed the craft coming toward his patrol car and quickly turned off the lights and pulled off the road.

Barton watched it carefully and pronounced it nothing he had ever seen before. "I was a military brat—my father was active-duty Air Force—so I'm familiar with both foreign and domestic aircraft," he says. "It got to where I could usually identify an aircraft just by the engine noise, and when this thing went over, it made zero noise . . . no noise whatsoever."[77]

Over the next several minutes Barton watched as the UFO turned, accelerating rapidly. Barton told his dispatcher to alert police officers in neighboring Shiloh, Millstadt, and Dupo, because the object would soon be visible in the skies over their towns. Soon the UFO was spotted by police in all three of those towns, and their descriptions matched that given by Barton.

The incident was investigated by independent science groups,

"QUOTE"

"I figure that there isn't much chance of our ever finding out what it was. And that's kind of sad, I think."

—A woman who saw a UFO while camping in the Boundary Waters of Minnesota in 2002.

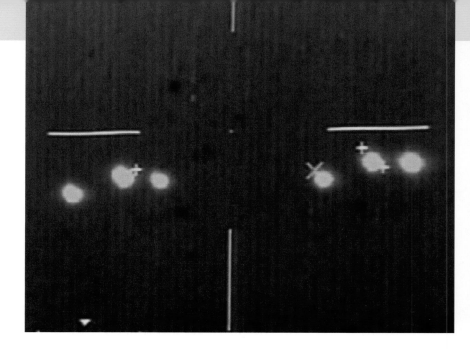

This video still made by the Mexican Air Force shows brightly lit, rapidly moving objects filmed on March 5, 2004 over Campeche, Mexico. One scientist stated that the lights could have been caused by a scientific phenomenon involving gases in the atmosphere.

such as the Seattle-based National UFO Reporting Center and the National Institute for Discovery Science (NIDS). In talking to officials at nearby Scott Air Force Base, investigators said no large aircraft of any kind were in the air at the time of the sightings and that nothing unusual showed on their radar. But all who witnessed the enormous UFO stuck to their stories. "Am I saying it was an alien spacecraft? No," said one of the police witnesses. "I'm not saying it was a military aircraft. I'm saying I can't identify the object."[78]

"The Lowest Form of Evidence"

While many investigators would be intrigued by the quality of the witnesses in the Illinois UFO sighting, for the vast majority of mainstream scientists such testimony is not compelling enough. Neil de Grasse Tyson, the director of New York City's Hayden Planetarium, says he is more than willing to listen to a sighting experience if it is accompanied by real artifacts. But he maintains that eyewitness testimony is never enough for a scientist.

"I don't care how many people say they've seen something—

they've seen lights in the sky," says Tyson. "As a scientist, I need something better than your eyewitness testimony. Even if in the court of law eyewitness testimony is a high form of evidence, in the court of science, it is the lowest form of evidence you could possibly put forth."[79]

Michael Shermer, the editor of *Skeptic* magazine, agrees wholeheartedly, saying the idea of a "quality witness" is meaningless. "It doesn't matter if it's President Jimmy Carter who saw a UFO—which he thinks he did—or Farmer Bob. It doesn't matter. Everybody has eyes and ears and a brain that perceives and so on. I think they're all equally unreliable as eyewitnesses. We're very bad at recounting things we think we saw."[80]

Looking in a Different Way

Although the scientific community is generally negative about reports of UFOs visiting Earth, it does not deny the possibility of extraterrestrial life. Some of the those who are most skeptical about UFOs do believe that intelligent life exists elsewhere in the universe.

Tyson says it is arrogant to believe otherwise, considering the almost inconceivably immense size of the universe. "There are more than a billion stars in our Milky Way galaxy alone," he says, "and more than 50 or 100 billion galaxies in the universe. You multiply those two numbers and that's a 1 with 22 zeroes worth of stars in the cosmos. To suggest that we're alone is inexcusably egocentric."[81]

Despite this view, scientists are still developing the tools by which such life can be detected. Efforts to develop these tools, many experts say, are more worthwhile than continually investigating UFO sightings and abductions.

Charlie, a graduate physics student from Illinois, says that such prioritizing makes good sense. "I look at it as being proactive," he says.

> Why should science just sit around on their hands waiting for [a UFO sighting] to occur so we can study it? Or, more likely, not study it, since there are so few shreds of helpful evidence. It makes a lot more sense to find other kinds of evidence of [extraterrestrial] life.
>
> My biggest hero is [astronomer and author] Carl Sagan. When talking about things like alien abduction, or UFOs, or anything like that, he used the sentence, "Extraordinary claims require extraordinary evidence." I know Sagan [who died in 1999] would have been the happiest man in the universe if he'd been shown real proof of a UFO. But the extraordinary evidence is not there yet. So really, I think science should devote itself to looking elsewhere for that sort of proof.[82]

Listening In

The search for one type of extraordinary proof was begun by Carl Sagan himself, as well as a number of other astronomers. Sagan felt strongly that any planet with intelligent life would be searching for other life in the universe, perhaps by sending radio waves into space. (Radio waves can travel extremely long distances.) Sagan believed that by aiming high-powered radio telescopes into outer space, Earth scientists might someday be able to pick up transmissions from other planets. This would be incontrovertible proof of intelligent life in the cosmos.

Radio waves have been sought for years, but a new facility in Hat Creek, California, about 300 miles (482km) north of San Francisco, can monitor those waves better than any other facility on Earth. An array of 350 high-powered radio receivers was built by a scientific organization called the SETI Institute (short for Search for Extraterrestrial Intelligence) in collaboration with the University of California at Berkeley. The receivers will scan the cosmos seven days a week, 24 hours a day for signals.

Seth Shostek, director of the SETI Institute, says that the facility may open up a whole new world for scientists, not only because of the number of its radio telescopes but the range of frequencies they can monitor. "We don't know how many civilizations out there might be broadcasting signals that we could pick up," he says. "The faster you can go through all that heavenly real estate, the sooner your going to find a signal. . . . This is the place where we're going to crack the crystal of isolation that has surrounded this planet for four and a half billion years."[83]

Protest from UFO Believers

But while such an undertaking is exciting to many scientists, many who believe strongly that UFOs have already visited Earth feel that it is a waste of time. Why spend billions of dollars on trying to find proof of life in the universe, they say, when there are hundreds—perhaps thousands—of people on Earth who are eyewitnesses to that fact? People have not only seen UFOs but have had contact with—and have on occasion been abducted by—aliens. Surely, such exploration is hardly necessary.

Writes Harold Egeln of *Close Encounter News*, "While SETI researchers tune in their radio telescopes, like children a few

Some believers in UFOs think that the Milky Way galaxy is simply too large for us to possibly be alone, or that other galaxies are so far away that it would be impossible to even know humans exist.

generations ago once did with their crystal radio playsets, hoping for the definite otherworldly radio or TV signal . . . witnesses are experiencing contact without benefit of cosmic radio receivers, providing [a] living database.[84]

Noted British ufologist John Spencer feels the same way and says scientists seem to be contradicting themselves. "Although mainstream, conventional scientists are not willing to accept the existence of a UFO phenomenon and therefore the possibility of extraterrestrials visiting the earth," he notes, "they appear perfectly prepared to accept the possibility of their existence."[85]

A 73,000-Year Trip?

But some scientists counter that the apparent contradiction lies in an issue that the UFO believers have not addressed. If indeed there have been the sightings they claim, how is it that aliens are able to travel to Earth with such apparent ease? Forget, they say, about the lack of real evidence from alleged sightings and

"A Present from a Small, Distant World"

The two Voyager space probes launched by NASA in 1977 carried tools for scientific research and for communicating with extraterrestrial life. Each probe held a special golden phonograph record intended for aliens—or even humans who may find it in the distant future. The Voyager crafts will take nearly 40,000 years to arrive at another star, so "future" is really quite distant. Included on the record is a greeting from then President Jimmy Carter, saying, "This is a present from a small, distant world, a token of our sounds, our science, our images, our music, our thoughts, and our feelings."

Also included are 115 different images and sounds, some natural, such as wind, birds, and whale songs; others human-made, ranging from Peruvian wedding songs to Scottish bagpipes, from Navajo night chants to slide guitar blues by Blind Willie Johnson. There are also samples of 55 spoken languages contained on the record, as well as detailed diagrams for playing it.

Quoted in "Howdy, Stranger,'" NASA homepage, August 19, 2002. www.nasa.gov.

abductions. What about the virtual impossibility of space travel from some far-away planet to Earth?

Albert Einstein calculated that nothing in the universe could travel faster than light—which is 186,000 miles (299,338km) per second. However, the fastest vehicle ever created by Earth scientists, the Voyager spacecraft, has a top speed of 11 miles (7km) per second. At that rate, it would take Voyager 73,000 years of top speed, 24-hours-per-day travel just to reach the nearest star outside Earth's solar system.

Obviously, no one could make the trip—and that is to the closest star. "Scientifically, we have a rule," says Tyson. "You want to be alive at the end of your experiment. Not dead. So if you're going to be a part of a space expedition, you want to get there faster than your life span."[86] And, say scientists, unless aliens have a life span of tens of thousands of years, they, too, would face the same problems.

Having a More Open Mind

But there are some scientists who are willing to entertain the idea of UFO visits. One of these is Michio Kaku. He is one of the top theoretical physicists in the world. Kaku has proposed an answer to the question of space travel. He says that a mistake many skeptics make in talking about intelligent life in the universe is in assuming such a civilization is similar to Earth in terms of technological know-how—perhaps ahead of Earth scientists by a few hundred years.

Kaku says that scientists should open themselves up to the idea that instead of being two hundred years ahead, such alien technology could be a great deal farther along. "Some people slam the door on the question of other civilizations visiting the earth because distances are so far away," he says. "I say, not so fast. . . . You simply cannot dismiss the possibility that some of these UFO sightings are actually sightings of some object created by some advanced civilization—a civilization far out in space, a civilization perhaps millions of years ahead of us in technology. You simply cannot discount that possibility."[87]

He suggests that such a civilization may have learned to use what Earth scientists are just thinking about today—shortcuts from one part of the universe to another. Known as "wormholes," these shortcuts are believed to exist in places where space has become warped, or distorted because of the energy around it. When that distortion becomes extreme, scientists say, two points that are in reality very far from one another are pushed closer together, forming a sort of tunnel. A space traveler who could navigate such wormholes would actually be able to turn a trip that might take million of years into one that takes only a few days. And maybe that is exactly what some alien civilization is doing.

Too Important to Ignore

Kaku is one of a few well-known and respected scientists who say that the existence of UFOs is far too important a possibility for science to ignore. Not only would it answer questions about life on other planets, but it could enable scientists on Earth to find solutions to the constraints of space travel. Perhaps, say some scientists, it is important to address the issue with all of the tools and energy modern science has at its disposal. "Maybe there's nothing there," Kaku says. "However, on that off chance that there is something there, that could literally change the course of human history. . . . I say, let this investigation begin."[88]

NOTES

Introduction: Not Alone

1. Val, personal interview by author, Minneapolis, Minnesota, March 4, 2007.
2. Quoted in Jon Hilkevitch, "In the Sky! A Bird? A Plane? A . . . UFO?" *Chicago Tribune*, January 1, 2007, p. 1A.
3. Quoted in Hilkevitch, "In the Sky!" p. 1A.
4. Val, interview.
5. Quoted in Hilkevitch, "In the Sky!" p. 1A.
6. Quoted in Lisa Faught, "It's Out There, People," *Orange Country* (CA) *Register*, July 6, 2000, p. 1.
7. Ali, personal interview by author, Minneapolis, Minnesota, February 4, 2007.

Chapter 1: Seeing Fire in the Skies

8. Quoted in Editors of Time-Life, *The UFO Phenomenon*. New York: Barnes and Noble, 1987, p. 12.
9. Quoted in Peter Brookesmith, *UFO: The Complete Sightings*. New York: Barnes and Noble, 1995, p. 14.
10. Quoted in Brookesmith, *UFO: The Complete Sightings*, p. 13.
11. Quoted in Editors of Time-Life, *The UFO Phenomenon*, pp. 12, 14.
12. Quoted in Editors of Time-Life, *The UFO Phenomenon*, p. 14.
13. Quoted in John Spencer and Anne Spencer, *Fifty Years of UFOs: From Distant Sightings to Close Encounters*. London: Boxtree, p. 12.
14. Quoted in Spencer and Spencer, *Fifty Years of UFOs*, p. 13.
15. Editors of Time-Life, *The UFO Phenomenon*, p. 38.

16. Quoted in Editors of Time-Life, *The UFO Phenomenon*, p. 38.
17. Editors of Time-Life, *Alien Encounters*. Alexandria, VA: Time-Life, 1992, p. 25.
18. Quoted in Spencer and Spencer, *Fifty Years of UFOs*, p. 25.
19. Quoted in Peter Carlson, "50 Years Ago, Unidentified Flying Objects from Way Beyond the Beltway Seize the Capital's Imagination," *Washington Post*, July 21, 2002, p. F1.
20. Quoted in Spencer and Spencer, *Fifty Years of UFOs*, p. 21.
21. Quoted in Carlson, "50 Years Ago," p. F1.
22. Quoted in Carlson, "50 Years Ago," p. F1.
23. Quoted in Editors of Time-Life, *The UFO Phenomenon*, p. 53.
24. Sandy, personal interview by author, St. Paul, Minnesota, March 13, 2007.

Chapter 2: UFOs and Roswell

25. Quoted in *Roswell Daily Record*, Roswell Files.com, July 8, 1947. www.roswellfiles.com.
26. Quoted in Editors of Time-Life, *The UFO Phenomenon*, p. 81.
27. Quoted in ABC News, "Seeing Is Believing," February 2005. www.abcnews.com.
28. Quoted in Peter Brookesmith, *UFO: The Government Files*. New York: Barnes and Noble, 1996, p. 148.
29. Quoted in Spencer and Spencer, *Fifty Years of UFOs*, p. 103.
30. Quoted in Editors of Time-Life, *Alien Encounters*, p. 79.
31. Quoted in QSL.net, "The Roswell Incident."

www.qsl.net.

32. Quoted in Kevin Randle, "Roswell Explained—Again," *Fate*, September 2005, p. 12.

33. Quoted in Editors of Time-Life, *The UFO Phenomenon*, p. 74.

34. Quoted in Editors of Time-Life, *The UFO Phenomenon*, p. 83.

35. Quoted in Karl T. Pflock, *Roswell: Inconvenient Facts and the Will to Believe.* Amherst, NY: Prometheus, 2001, p. 31.

36. Quoted in Editors of Time-Life, *The UFO Phenomenon*, p. 85.

37. Quoted in Editors of Time-Life, *The UFO Phenomenon*, p. 85.

38. Quoted in Pflock, *Roswell*, p. 131.

39. Quoted in Lana Berkowitz, "Extraterrestrial Encounters: Fact or Fantasy?" *Houston Chronicle*, June 26, 2005, p. J1.

Chapter 3: New Kinds of Proof

40. Quoted in James Randi, *Flim-Flam! Psychics, Unicorns, and Other Delusions.* New York: Prometheus, 1982, p. 87.

41. Quoted in About.com, "1980: The Cash/Landrum Piney Woods Encounter." http://ufos.about.com.

42. Quoted in Spencer and Spencer, *Fifty Years of UFOs*, p. 86.

43. Quoted in *UFO Casefiles*, "1971: The Delphos, Kansas UFO Landing Ring." www.ufocasebook.com.

44. Quoted in *UFO Casefiles*, "1971: The Delphos, Kansas UFO Landing Ring."

45. Mark Davidson, personal interview by author, Minneapolis, Minnesota, February 7, 2007.

46. Quoted in UFO Evidence, "Renato Nicolai." www.ufoevidence.org.

47. Quoted in UFO Evidence, "UFO Case Report: Trans-en-Provence Physical Trace Case." www.ufoevidence.org.

48. Quoted in UFO Evidence, "UFO Case Report: Trans-en-Provence."

49. Quoted in Freddy Silva, "A Brief Education on Crop Circles," UFO Evidence. www.ufoevidence.org.

50. Quoted in Silva, "A Brief Education on Crop Circles."

51. Quoted in Scott Corrales, "Enter the Mutilators," *Fate*, September 2005, p. 24.

52. Quoted in Corrales, "Enter the Mutilators," p. 27.

Chapter 4: Alien Abductions

53. Quoted in Milan Wall, "Ashland Officer Makes Routine Report on UFO." http://msnusers.com.

54. Quoted in Wall, "Ashland Officer Makes Routine Report on UFO."

55. Quoted in Editors of Time-Life, *The UFO Phenomenon*, p. 82.

56. Quoted in Editors of Time-Life, *The UFO Phenomenon*, p. 48.

57. Quoted in John G. Fuller, *The Interrupted Journey: Two Lost Hours "Aboard a Flying Saucer."* New York: Dial, 1966, p. 164.

58. Quoted in Editors of Time-Life, *The UFO Phenomenon*, p. 82.

59. Editors of Time-Life, *The UFO Phenomenon*, p. 143.

60. Quoted in UFO Folklore Center, "Implants Removed!" www.artgomperz.com.

61. Quoted in Peter Brookesmith, *Alien Abductions.* New York: Barnes and Noble, 1998, p. 94.

62. Quoted in Wall, "Ashland Officer Makes Routine Report on UFOs."

63. Quoted in Michael Lucas, "Venturing from Shadows into Light," *Los Angeles Times*, September 4, 2001, p. E2.

64. Quoted in ABC News, "UFOs: Seeing Is Believing."

65. Jeanne, telephone interview by author, March 16, 2007.

66. Lynn, telephone interview by author, March 1, 2007.
67. Lynn, telephone interview.
68. Quoted in David Derbyshire, "Alien Abduction Stories Brought Down to Earth," *Daily* (London) *Telegraph*, February 18, 2003, p. 10.
69. Quoted in ABC News, "UFOs: Seeing Is Believing."
70. Quoted in Lucas, "Venturing from Shadows into Light," p. E2.

Chapter 5:
"I Say, Let this Investigation Begin"

71. Lorraine, personal interview by author, Minneapolis, Minnesota, February 21, 2007.
72. Quoted in Lianne Hart, "Treasure Trove of UFO Data Lands at a Texas University," *Los Angeles Times*, November 2, 2003, p. A33.
73. Quoted in Hart, "Treasure Trove of UFO Data," p. A33.
74. Quoted in Peter N. Spotts, "Scientists' New Spin on UFOs," *Christian Science Monitor*, June 25, 1998, p. 1.
75. Quoted in Spotts, "Scientists' New Spin," p. 1.
76. Quoted in UFO Evidence, "Space Case: Witnesses Testify in the Mystery of the Metro East UFO." www.ufoevidence.org.
77. Quoted in UFO Evidence, "Space Case."
78. Quoted in ABC News, "UFOs: Seeing Is Believing."
79. Quoted in Harold Egeln, "Experience Is Knowing: Beyond the ABC-TV UFO Special," *Close Encounters News.* http://community-2.wcbtv.net.
80. Quoted in *ABC News*, "UFOs: Seeing Is Believing."
81. Quoted in Egeln, "Experience Is Knowing."
82. Charlie, telephone interview by author, February 27, 2007.
83. Quoted in ABC News, "UFOs: Seeing Is Believing."
84. Egeln, "Experience Is Knowing."
85. John Spencer, *The UFO Encyclopedia.* New York: Avon, 1991, p. 276.
86. Quoted in ABC News, "UFOs: Seeing Is Believing."
87. Quoted in ABC News, "UFOs: Seeing Is Believing."
88. Quoted in *UFO Digest*, "UFO Technology Could Provide Climate Change Solutions: Former Canadian Defense Minister," February 26, 2007. www.ufodigest.com.

For Further Research

Books

Karen Condon, ed., *UFOs*. San Diego: Greenhaven, 2005. An interesting assortment of articles by both skeptics and believers in the UFO phenomenon. Especially interesting are the two articles giving the pros and cons about alien abductions.

Jay Goldner, *Messages from Space: Crop Circles Bring the First Indisputable Extraterrestrial Signs From Space*. Studio City, CA: Michael Wiese Productions, 2002. Very complete information the intricacies of crop circles; excellent maps.

Kenneth Randle, *Invasion Washington: UFOs over the Capitol*. New York: HarperCollins, 2001. Excellent quotes from a variety of sources; very readable.

Kenneth Randle, Russ Estes, and William P. Cone, *The Abduction Engima*. New York: Tom Doherty Associates, 1999. The result of thousands of hours of taped interviews with victims of alien abduction, this book—although a bit old—is extremely interesting. Good bibliography is included.

Periodicals

Steve Connor, "Why Being Abducted Can Seem So Real," *Independent* (London), February 18, 2003.

Michelle Hunter, "Eyes on the Skies," *New Orleans Times-Picayune*, July 1, 2004.

Diana Jean Schemo, "Harvard Advertises for People Abducted by Aliens, but the Truth Is Out There a Little Farther," *New York Times*, December 18, 2002.

Web Sites

Golden Record (www.goldenrecord.org/sounds.htm).

This is an excellent multimedia guide to the music, images, and greetings NASA has sent on the Voyager 1 and 2 space probes, hoping to give any aliens an idea of what Earth is like.

Historical Artwork and UFOs (www.ufoartwork.com).

A fascinating compilation of art going back to prehistoric days that seems to show UFOs in the background of paintings.

Mutual UFO Network (www.mufon.com).

The Mutual UFO Network is an independent scientific organization dedicated to studying reports of UFO sightings. The Web site gives a great deal of information about the most interesting UFO sightings in history, advice for people who see a UFO, and links to other UFO organizations.

SETI Institute (www.seti.org).

This is the Web site of the Search for Extraterrestrial Intelligence Institute. It contains a great deal of information about ongoing projects, including a virtual visit to the new telescope array.

UFO Evidence (www.ufoevidence.org).

This is the Internet's largest site for information, photographs, and discussions of current UFO sightings and reports, as well as fascinating glimpses into the science of investigating UFOs.

NDEX

ABOUT THE AUTHOR

Gail B. Stewart is the author of more than 200 books for children and young adults. She lives in Minneapolis with her husband, 2 dogs, and a cat. She has 3 grown sons.